To

Congregation Beth Shalom
with great admiration and
very best wishes.
Adam Starkopf
4/28-2003.

WILL TO LIVE

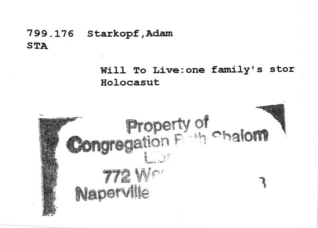

WILL TO LIVE

One Family's Story of
Surviving the Holocaust

Adam Starkopf

STATE UNIVERSITY OF NEW YORK PRESS

Originally published under the title, *There is Always Time to Die* © 1981 by Adam Starkopf, Holocaust Library.

Published by
State University of New York Press, Albany

For information, address State University of New York Press,
90 State Street, Suite 700, Albany, NY 12207

Production by Marilyn P. Semerad
Marketing by Fran Keneston

Library of Congress Cataloging-in-Publication Data

Starkopf, Adam.
    [There is always time to die]
    Will to live : one family's story of surviving the Holocaust /
Adam Starkopf.
       p. cm.
    Originally published under the title: There is always time to die,
by Adam Starkopf, Holocaust Library, c1981.
    ISBN 0-7914-2619-X (hardcover : alk. paper). — ISBN 0-7914-2620-3
(pbk. : alk. paper)
    1. Jews—Persecutions—Poland—Warsaw. 2. Holocaust—Poland–
–Warsaw—Personal narratives. 3. Starkopf, Adam. 4. Warsaw
(Poland)—Ethnic relations. I. Title.
DS135.P62W364 1995
940.53'18'092—dc20
    [B]   95-33065
                                     CIP

10 9 8 7 6 5 4 3 2

Adam Starkopf, the author

FOREWORD

This is an extraordinary story. All Holocaust survivors' stories are extraordinary, but this one has a special tinge to it: parents who are motivated chiefly by the tremendous desire to save their child. Strokes of luck play their part; the so-called "Aryan" features of this very Jewish couple also play a part. But the main theme is courage, and a tremendous will to live. The journey takes the Starkopfs from Warsaw to the immediate vicinity of one of the most frightful places on earth—the death camp of Treblinka. They survive on false papers, on false identities, witnesses to the tragedy of millions.

The literature of memoirs is growing, and each addition is important. It will take a long time to sift and weigh and internalize. The memoirs of Pela and Adam Starkopf will form an important item in the collection, to be read and reread and imbibed by the generations yet to come.

Prof. Yehuda Bauer
Chairman, Institute of
  Contemporary Jewry
The Hebrew University
  of Jerusalem

THIS BOOK IS DEDICATED
TO THE EVERLASTING MEMORY
OF OUR BELOVED PARENTS
MIRIAM & MAX STARKOPF
AND
MIRIAM & AARON MILLER
AND OUR BROTHERS
HENRY STARKOPF & BEN (DOV) MILLER

1

At six o'clock in the morning of Friday, September 1, 1939, the news first came to us over the Polish State Radio. The German army had crossed the Polish border near the city of Bogumil the night before and our country was at war with Hitler's *Reich*.

The people of Warsaw lost their heads. They crowded into the grocery stores, desperate to buy up every last bit of food. Women formed lines several blocks long for bread to store in their cellars for the time when there would be nothing else to eat.

Just before noon the radio reported that our soldiers had repelled the German invaders. My knees went weak with relief. But minutes later reality intruded; even as the announcer proclaimed the incredible victory of Poland's armed forces the first German bombers appeared in the skies above Warsaw.

I was a young man then, twenty-five years old. I had been married three years and was earning a good salary as the office manager and chief accountant of a leather goods factory in Warsaw. Despite the commotion in the streets that day, I set out for my office. But no one seemed to be in the mood for work. We stood huddled in groups outside the factory building, discussing the situation and listening to the news reports that burst every few minutes from megaphones mounted to the walls of buildings nearby.

Two Polish policemen sauntered by. "Don't worry, don't worry," one of them said cheerfully. "Those planes up in the sky aren't German. They're ours. Polish." But even while the policeman grinned at us, we could hear the anti-aircraft batteries firing away.

I later learned that the first German bomb dropped near Warsaw had hit a Jewish children's sanatorium at Miedzeszyn, a health resort not far from Warsaw. The hospital sustained a direct hit and most of the children were killed.

After a while I went home to the apartment on Novolipki Street which my wife, Pela, and I shared with my parents. I found Pela and my mother in tears. We kept the radio on day and night. The news reports reflected Poland's woeful lack of preparedness. My own mood seesawed between excitement and apprehension because I expected to receive my draft notice at any moment.

Our orders came over the radio only the next day— Saturday, September 2. All able-bodied young men were instructed to report to their recruiting stations immediately. But when I arrived at my recruiting station I was sent home "until further notice." They said that their supply of uniforms had run out....

All over Poland, *Volksdeutsche* (Polish citizens of German descent) revealed themselves as traitors and saboteurs. Disguised in the tight black work costume of chimney sweeps they appeared on the roofs of Warsaw's apartment buildings, pretending to clean the chimneys while using their brooms to signal the low-flying German bombers.

At one point the Polish State Radio announced that the Germans were likely to drop gas bombs and informed us that the neighborhood civil defense committees would distribute gas masks to the public free of charge. But there were not enough gas masks to go around. So the drug stores sold gauze pads soaked in a chemical to hold in front of our noses and mouths in case the Germans really used gas. There was a run on the drug stores and soon it was no longer possible to get the gauze pads.

At home, my mother sat on our living room sofa, cutting gauze pads to size for the four of us, while the radio continued its announcements in a steady monotone. A bulletin came, advising every household to keep on hand one blanket for each person and to store as much water as possible in buckets. If the Germans used gas we should soak the blankets in the water and throw them over our heads for protection against the poisonous fumes.

The following day—Sunday, September 3—the radio announced that Great Britain and France had declared war on Germany and would come to Poland's rescue. Warsaw thrilled with renewed hope. There were demonstrations in front of the British and French embassies, with thousands of excited Poles belting out cheers for our brave allies.

But on Monday the mood plummeted once again. It was rumored that Poland's president, Ignacy Moscicki, and his cabinet had fled across the border to neutral Rumania, taking with them all the funds of the Polish government.

On Tuesday, September 5, Warsaw was bombed all day long. That evening, the janitor of our apartment building rang our doorbell with the latest orders from our neighborhood civil defense committee. Every able-bodied male was needed to dig trenches on the outskirts of Warsaw. Along with the other young men from our building, I set out for civil defense headquarters, but within an hour we were back home again: the civil defense committee did not have enough spades for us....

We stayed awake all that night, listening to the radio and looking out of the windows to scan the skies for German planes.

At one o'clock on Wednesday morning, September 6, Colonel Umiastowski of the General Staff Military Headquarters came on the air. All young men, he said, were to leave Warsaw and travel east to the city of Brzesc, where they would be supplied with uniforms and inducted into the army. He did not even mention the address or the authority to which he expected the young men to report when—and if—they got to Brzesc, some 120 miles east of Warsaw.

We spent the rest of the night discussing whether or not I should heed the Colonel's confused appeal. My father argued that since the Colonel had not issued any clear directives, I had better wait until more definite orders came through. While Father and I talked, my mother and Pela sat on the sofa side by side, in dazed silence. I was my parents' only son at home. My older brother, Henry, had left Poland six years earlier. Our family had never been particularly devout, but we had been caught up in the Zionist pioneering spirit that had swept Polish Jewry in the 1920's and 1930's. He went to Palestine with the Maccabi team on motorcycles to attend an international Jewish athletic meet. Once in Palestine, my brother and some of his friends "deserted" and, armed only with the short-term visitors' visas issued to them by the British authorities, managed to stay in the country. My brother found work as a construction laborer, carrying bricks to help rebuild the Jewish homeland. I might have gone to Palestine with him, but I had not done so because I was then already keeping company with Pela. We'd been childhood sweethearts.

Brzesc was not an unknown city to Pela and me. I had worked in Brzesc several months after our marriage, and both Pela and I had made good friends there during that time. But both our parents had been unhappy about our move; so we had returned to Warsaw. We did not know whether our friends were still in Brzesc. Father and I went for advice to our neighbors across the hall, our old friends, the Golds. Mr. Gold, like my father, had been in the leather goods business. The Golds had three sons. The older two—Jerzyk, who was 20, and Lutek, who was 18—were of draft age. The third and youngest, Rysio, was only 14. After a lively discussion in our apartment, it was decided that Jerzyk, Lutek and I should set out for Brzesc together. Rysio announced that he would go with us. He assured us that he could fight the Germans better than all the rest of us combined. Had our minds been functioning normally, his brothers and I certainly would have refused to take him with us, but we were so completely cut off from the realities of ordinary life and thought that not even Mrs. Gold raised any objections to Rysio's leaving.

At five o'clock in the morning Pela packed a knapsack for me with some food and a few changes of underwear. I wanted to carry as little with me as possible because I knew that traveling conditions would be chaotic and we would probably end up making most of our journey to Brzesc on foot. The one valuable possession I decided to take was my wrist watch. At the last moment, I removed a map of Poland from my desk drawer and stuffed it into my knapsack. It occurred to me that the map might come in handy.

The three Golds and I were joined by another neighbor, Mr. Kaplan, the editor of a Warsaw Yiddish newspaper, and his son Jerzyk, whom we called "Jerzyk II" to distinguish him from Jerzyk Gold and who had just graduated from gymnasium with the highest academic honors. Also with us were my good friend Edward Dolniak and his brother, who was only 17. A few more neighbors joined our group, but since they were not close friends of ours, I cannot recall their names now.

Just before I left our apartment, my father led me into his bedroom and stammered a few words of last-minute advice. Then he broke down in sobs. Finally, we kissed and parted in the lobby of the apartment building. My mother and Pela, both still in their slippers and housecoats, accompanied me out into the street, as far as the Kierbedz Bridge, which spanned the Vistula River and linked Warsaw with a suburb called Praga. At the bridge, I quickly embraced them both. Pela wept but my mother did her best to smile.

When I turned back for one last look at my wife and my mother, I saw Mother gently leading Pela away. I was never to see my mother again.

2

As our group—with the Gold brothers, the Kaplans and myself in the lead—crossed the Kierbedz Bridge into Praga, hell erupted above and around us. We were under almost constant machine-gun fire from German dive bombers. Every few minutes we had to get off the street and duck into the nearest building that was still intact. It took us over six hours to reach the Lublin highway, only four miles outside Praga.

The bombs kept falling. Buildings collapsed to the right and the left of us, and people dropped to the ground, torn by bombs or mowed down by machine-gun bullets.

When we finally came to the Lublin highway, which led to the city of Minsk-Mazowiecki, it was noon and the highway was blocked with refugees traveling on foot, in cars or in wagons laden with their possessions. The German planes were still overhead, dropping bombs and sputtering machine-gun bullets. We turned off the highway and took shelter in potato fields, throwing ourselves flat on the ground. Whenever there was a lull in the firing, we leaped to our feet and took a few more steps forward until the next round of shooting drove us off the road again. We passed human bodies that had been ripped apart, dead horses and cows, and the twisted, smoking remains of cars and wagons. The ceaseless rat-tat-tat of the German machine guns mingled with the roar of the German dive bombers and the cries of the wounded refugees.

I assumed command of our group. Not all the neighbors who had come with us were Jews. I am not even so sure that they liked the Jews, but now that we all were facing the same danger, both they and we forgot the differences that had separated us before the war.

On that first day of flight we kept moving until late in the evening. I led our group along the side roads because the main highway seemed to be the hardest hit by the bombs and machine guns. On that day we covered altogether 25 miles, but to me it felt like at least 150. By nightfall, some of our neighbors had had enough. They announced that they were heading back for Warsaw. "You'll never make it to Brzesc. You'll be killed before you ever get there," they said as they bade us good-by.

As night fell, we saw refugees leaving the highways to look for farms at which to spend the night. Some sought shelter in the woods. But I suggested that we should take advantage of the darkness, when the machine-gun fire would not be so heavy, and continue marching through the night.

None of us had any weapons. We believed that once we were inducted into the army in Brzesc, we would be given weapons along with our uniforms. However, Brzesc was still hundred miles away. Somewhere on the highway I found an automatic revolver lying on the ground. Probably it had been dropped there by a refugee—or perhaps by a Polish deserter. At any rate, I picked up the gun and slipped it into my belt.

We traveled for five days, stopping again and again to seek cover from the German bombs and bullets. By that time our food supplies had run out and we were hungry and thirsty, but there was no way for us to get food or even water, because the villages along the highway had been reduced to rubble by German bombs or abandoned by their terrified inhabitants. It seemed that even the wayside wells had run dry.

At the end of five days we had covered about sixty miles, or half the way from Warsaw to Brzesc. The bombing and machine-gunning continued without letup. The German bombers roamed the skies at will; the Polish anti-aircraft defenses had fallen silent. After five days on the road, our feet were sore and each step was agony; yet we felt we were better off than the refugees who were traveling in cars or horse-drawn wagons. You could make much better time on the clogged highways if you traveled on foot; it gave you more freedom of movement. It was also safer because you could dash for shelter in the fields or woods in a matter of seconds.

At midnight on September 11 we passed through Siedlce. The city was ablaze under the German bombing. Smoke seared our eyes and throats and our clothes caught fire from the cinders that kept dropping from the burning houses.

I was worried about the editor Kaplan and his son, "Jerzyk II." They both seemed physically and mentally exhausted, so much so that they had thrown away their knapsacks. The three Gold brothers, Jerzyk, Lutek and even young Rysio, on the other hand, were still in pretty good shape, laughing and joking.

Every time we stopped for a rest, and again before resuming our march, I made a roll call. During the first five days of our journey, we had been lucky; we had suffered no casualties. But now, as we made our way through Siedlce, we lost two men, whose names I do not remember. Hit by shrapnel, they were killed instantly.

By September 13 the German bombing and machine-gunning had abated because we were now some distance away from the battle-front. We turned off the highway into the woods intending to take a long rest—perhaps our first spell of real quiet since we had started out from Warsaw. We lay down in the damp grass and discussed the next stage of our journey to Brzesc. Refugees we had met on the highway told us that the Germans had established bases at several points only 20 miles away from where we were. I pulled from my knapsack the map I had brought with me from Warsaw and tried to work out a route which would by-pass the Germans. As I, and a few others, bent over the map, we were startled by the drone of an airplane engine close by. We leaped to our feet. We saw a clearing, and there was a small, two-engine plane, just taking off from the ground. It bore the markings of the German *Luftwaffe*. Standing nearby, motionless, apparently watching the plane take off, was a man wearing the uniform and insignia of a lieutenant in the Polish army. I thought it was strange that a Polish officer should have managed to get so close to a German plane without being caught. I released the safety catch of my newly-acquired revolver and told the other men that if I gave them a signal they should leap out from behind the trees and overpower the lieutenant. Then, my gun hidden from view, I approached the officer. I struck the pose of an innocent country yokel. "Mister Lieutenant," I asked him, "what are you doing here? Wasn't that a German plane that just took off?" His answer came in an excellent Polish, with no trace of a foreign accent. "Yes, those damned Germans do seem to be everywhere, don't they? We can't get away from them, can we?"

17

Before I could say or do anything in reply, we were surrounded by Polish soldiers. The lieutenant never had a chance, for a Polish sergeant took away his gun and ordered his men to search him. The lieutenant turned out to have on his person three other guns, several German documents and a map of the entire region. When the sergeant interrogated him, he admitted that he was not a Polish soldier but an officer in the German army. Disguised in a Polish uniform, he had been deposited in the clearing by the German plane which had just left, with orders to inform the Germans about Polish troop and civilian movements in the area. Like the make-believe chimney-sweeps in Warsaw, this lieutenant was a *Volksdeutscher* who had been born and educated in Poland, so that he had had no trouble passing as a Pole. But now his luck had run out, for after the interrogation the sergeant put an end to his life with one well-aimed bullet.

That evening, our group broke up. The three Gold brothers and the two Kaplans were not happy with the travel route I had chosen. They took my map and argued that they knew a much better and faster way of getting to Brzesc. I explained to them that the route they suggested was dangerously close to territory already occupied by the Germans, and that by the time we would arrive there, the Germans might well be in complete command. I knew what I was talking about because I was thoroughly familiar with the terrain. But the Golds and the Kaplans remained adamant and declared that they would rather return to Warsaw than continue traveling with us. As I was to learn later, only Lutek and Jerzyk Gold made it back to Warsaw; their brother Rysio and the Kaplans fell into the hands of the Germans on the way and were killed.

Those of us who were left—the Dolniak brothers, several other neighbors from our apartment block, and

I—accepted a lift from a unit of cadets from an officers' training school who were lumbering along the highway in horse-drawn wagons. It was a vast relief. For the first time in eight days I did not have to travel on foot. After our 100-mile trek east from Warsaw, my shoes were torn to shreds. The soles had been flapping loose and I had tied them to my feet with pieces of coarse rope I had picked up somewhere on the road. My feet were badly swollen and inflamed; every step was torture. My throat was dry, but there was no water anywhere to drink.

At about midnight our wagon train came to a halt because all the roads were blocked with refugees. It was now impossible to move even an inch. However, the shooting had stopped. Also, we felt that we were no longer alone; we had the Polish cadets to protect us now.

Suddenly, there was the crack of a single carbine shot, followed by a hail of bullets from behind the trees on both sides of the highway. We jumped off the wagons and leaped into the ditches that lined the highway on either side, but the ditches were not deep enough to provide shelter from the crossfire. The cadets started to shoot from the ditches in either direction but the bullets from the woods kept whizzing through the air and within minutes many of the cadets had toppled to the ground, dead or wounded.

I think that at this point I lost my head. I scrambled to my feet and climbed out of my ditch, zigzagging across the field behind the ditch, toward the woods from where the bullets were still coming. A few of the surviving cadets rushed after me. Every few seconds we had to fling ourselves flat on the ground to dodge the bullets. Then we got up again and resumed our race for the woods. I had finally thrown away my knapsack, but I still had my revolver. It was loaded, and I was determined to put it to good use if I got caught by the Germans. I would shoot as many Germans as I could, but I would make sure to save one bullet for myself because I had no illusions about being able to fend off the Germans single-handedly and it did not require much imagination to picture what the Germans would do to me, especially once they found out that I was Jewish.

The 200 yards that separated the side of the highway from the sheltering woods seemed like 200 miles, but I managed to avoid the bullets and to reach the woods unharmed. I leaped into a cluster of bushes at the edge of the woods and lay there quite still, afraid to move. I think that the crossfire above my head must have continued for at least another hour before it finally stopped.

As I lay in the bushes I heard a noise that sounded like the call of a cuckoo. This was followed by a half-hiccupping, half-sobbing sound, like the cry of a baby. After a moment of stunned surprise, it dawned upon me that these weird sounds were signals exchanged by *Volksdeutsche* and Polish subversives trying to finish the mopping-up operations which the advancing German army had left for them to complete: to kill as many Poles as possible and to create chaos behind the fighting lines.

Then came a rustle from the bushes, followed by the muffled sound of footsteps. I lay flat on my stomach, hugged the ground and held my breath. Then, cautiously, I raised my head. There was a German soldier wearing a steel helmet, a machine gun slung casually over his shoulder. He kept looking to the right and to the left, and at one point walked right past me. My first impulse was to expend one of the precious bullets in my revolver to finish him off. But then it occurred to me that I would have little to gain from killing just one German, and everything to lose, because if this one German was here, there had to be plenty of others close by, and I would not stand a chance. So I stayed where I was, neither moving nor making a sound. After a while, the German turned on his heel and disappeared.

I wondered what I should do: run back to the highway while it was still dark, or wait another few hours until the sun would rise? I decided to wait. At dawn, wet and thoroughly chilled from lying in the damp grass, I inched, on my hands and knees, toward the field that lay between the woods and the highway. I remember that the green fields were stained red with blood. The fields and the highway were littered with dead horses and human bodies. Here and there I saw wounded—some in Polish uniform, others in civilian clothing. Several Polish soldiers appeared. They stopped and I helped them load the wounded onto the trucks, wagons and ambulances that crept along the highway.

I found several cadets, and eventually also the two Dolniaks, lying in a ditch, badly scared but otherwise unhurt. The other neighbors who had stayed with us after the Golds and the Kaplans had left were gone. Later, I came upon a few of them; they were stretched out on the ground, dead. As I bent over one of the bodies, I remembered how, back in Warsaw, that man's wife had clung to his arm and begged him not to leave her.

Miraculously, the wagons we had abandoned during the night were still at the place where we had left them; so were the horses. The Dolniaks, the surviving Polish cadets and I climbed into the wagons and continued the journey to Brzesc.

3

At about 3 o'clock in the morning of Friday, September 15—the eve of Rosh HaShanah, the Jewish New Year—we arrived in Brzesc. The city was a mass of flames. The bridge over the River Bug had been destroyed and had been replaced by a makeshift pontoon. There was no point in inquiring about an induction center, much less about our friends. Soldiers and civilians were streaming out of the city. The Dolniaks and I somehow became separated from the cadets. We were sure that the Germans would be in Brzesc in a matter of hours. The three of us gingerly made our way through the rubble-strewn streets in the direction of the railroad station. We had picked up rumors that an eastbound army freight train would be leaving shortly for Baranowicze, a city near the border of the Soviet Union, where the Polish army was supposed to be regrouping for a massive westward offensive to drive the Germans back.

As we neared the station—or what was left of it— German planes appeared in the sky above us and started dropping bombs. One bomb exploded not far from us. I felt a sharp, searing pain in my foot. The pain stopped me, but only for a moment. Then I continued running. But suddenly, much to my surprise, I realized that I was lying on the ground. I had been hit in the foot, near the toes, by a small piece of shrapnel. The two Dolniaks panicked; they did not know how to help me. I begged them to leave me where I was and to save themselves, but they would not hear of it. I took off my khaki shirt and tore a strip from it to bandage my foot. I was bleeding heavily and my whole foot throbbed with pain. No one else seemed to see us; everyone was too busy trying to save his own life. The two Dolniaks half-led, half-carried me to the ruins of a bombed-out building. "Stay here," said Edward, "We'll see if we can't find somebody to look at your wound."

Hours went by, with no sign of the Dolniaks. I was sure that they had been killed, that the Germans would arrive at any moment, and that my end had come. But at about 9 o'clock an ambulance came to a stop directly in front of me. A medic emerged, followed by the Dolniaks. Together, the three carried me into the ambulance. Later, the Dolniaks explained that they had gotten lost in the city and had been unable to retrace their way to the place where they had left me. But luckily they had come upon the ambulance and the medic had helped them find me.

Inside the ambulance, the medic unwound the primitive bandage from my foot. Then, without an anaesthetic, he calmly proceeded to amputate one of my toes. He explained that he had to do this in order to save my leg. "This is no time to lose your nerve, young man," he said to me as he worked on my foot. "It would be a pity for you to die so soon." I saw a shower of stars before my eyes, and I think I lost consciousness. When I became aware of my surroundings again, I was glad to see that, at least, I still had my foot, and I thanked the medic warmly. The Dolniaks wanted to remove me from the ambulance but the medic insisted on driving us to the railroad station. He told us that he had been instructed to drive his ambulance aboard the next eastbound train. The Polish army would need his ambulance, he said, "for the counterattack."

At the station, the ambulance—with the medic, the Dolniaks and myself aboard—was loaded onto an open freight car. With a little help from the Dolniaks, I crawled out of the ambulance and eased myself onto the floor of the freight car, where others, obviously refugees, had already settled down for the journey.

By that time the pain in my foot had been almost blanked out by a feeling of dark despair. I was sure that even if I survived the next few days, I would never see Pela or my parents again. Mercifully, at this point, the medic gave me a sleeping pill. I spent the rest of the journey in a daze. Several times, German bombers roared low overhead. Each time this happened, the train jerked to a stop and everyone jumped out to take cover in the fields on either side of the tracks, but I did not have the strength to move from my place. However, luck was with me once again: the train was not hit.

We pulled into Baranowicze during the night of September 15. Since Baranowicze was only about 50 kilometers from the Soviet border, I thought we should be safe there. But when we got off our train, we learned that the first German bombs had already fallen upon Baranowicze.

One of the refugees mentioned the town of Kletzk, about 42 kilometers east of Baranowicze and only seven or eight kilometers from the border. Supposedly, things were still quiet there. About fifteen of the refugees from the freight train, including the Dolniaks and myself, decided that we should not waste a minute in Baranowicze but move on to Kletzk at once. Somehow, we found a horse and wagon. We climbed aboard, paid the driver and persuaded him to take us to Kletzk.

It turned out to be the right decision. Kletzk was still so calm and peaceful that one could hardly believe there was a war going on. The people of the town said they had never even seen a German plane. I thought that this was odd.

We asked someone to direct us to the town hall. The town council took charge of us at once. I was taken to a small clinic where my foot was treated and bandaged properly. I was incredibly filthy; my clothes hung from me in tatters and the last time I shaved had been in Warsaw, more than two weeks earlier. We were assigned to a local family who gave us food and some clean clothes. They put us up for the night in a very clean, fresh-smelling barn. We spent that night on scratchy hay, but to me it felt as soft as a bed of goosedown feathers. Yet it took me a long time before I could sleep. It was now the second night of Rosh HaShanah, when Jewish families should be together to welcome their New Year, but I was hundreds of miles away from my loved ones. I was safe, at least for the time being, but what about Pela and our parents? Were they still alive? Would I ever see them again?

Early the next morning I was awakened from a fitful sleep by the drone of planes flying very low and the thunder of tanks rumbling over the highway outside the barn. I quickly got up—I had slept with all my clothes on—and hobbled out of the barn. I sat down on a tree stump and looked out upon the highway. I could not believe what I saw.

An endless column of artillery, tanks, trucks and armored cars came rolling along the highway from the east. At first I saw neither soldiers nor national emblems. What was this? Had the Germans caught up with us? But it could not be the Germans, I told myself; the Germans would have to come from the west, not from the east. It must be the Russians, then. At that moment the turret of one of the passing tanks opened, and a face appeared with a broad grin, flashing a row of silver teeth. With those teeth, this had to be a Russian! Only then did I notice that the tanks bore the Red Star, the hammer and sickle, and the letters U-S-S-R.

By this time the others who had made the journey from Baranowicze had emerged from the barn and we stood staring at the awesome display of Soviet weaponry. A couple of Russians jumped from a truck, pumped our hands and shouted "Zdrastvuite"—"Hello, there!"

I was ecstatic. So the Russians were moving west to help the Poles push back the Germans! But I was soon disillusioned. Our hosts learned the truth and made no effort to keep it from us. The Polish soldiers and police who had been stationed in Kletzk had fled during the night. The Russians had captured some of them and were now taking them away as prisoners of war. At last, I understood. The Russians were occupying Kletzk not as our liberators but under a peaceful arrangement with the Germans: the Russians and the Germans were operating hand in hand, amicably dividing Poland between themselves. This was the reason why the German bombers had stayed away from Kletzk and other areas near the border of the USSR.

I accepted this new reality with mixed emotions: relief that I had not fallen into the hands of the Germans, but anguish at the thought that the formal partition of Poland between Germany and the Soviet Union might separate me forever from my loved ones in Warsaw. I was seized with such a desperate longing for Pela and my parents that I no longer cared what might happen to me. All I wanted was to get back to Warsaw as quickly as possible, to be with my family before the borders between the German and Russian sectors of Poland would be sealed for good.

Slowly, I went back into the barn. My self-control gave way and, for the first time since I left home, I burst into tears. But then I pulled myself together. As long as I was alive, I told myself, I must not give up hope. Above all, I must not do anything rash that would endanger my own life without helping my family.

I left the barn and walked through the town. I could feel the excitement and tension in the air. Some of the people whom I passed were smiling broadly; others looked uncertain and apprehensive.

I made up my mind to stay in Kletzk for the time being. I learned that food was still available in the town, so that it would be possible for me to survive. True, the few zlotys I had brought with me from Warsaw were almost gone, but I still had with me my wrist watch, which I had been saving for a time like this.

As the days passed, my wound began to heal and I was able to move about more. As I walked through the streets of Kletzk, I tried to think of a way to contact my family in Warsaw, but I could find none.

On Sunday, September 24—it was the eve of Yom Kippur, the most solemn of the Jewish High Holidays— as I was walking through a street near the town's market place, I was seized by two uniformed Russians and placed under arrest. The Russians had been patrolling the streets of Kletzk, looking for Polish deserters. With my blond hair, blue eyes, fair complexion and military gait, I had attracted their attention. Although my papers were in order, the Russians insisted that I was a Polish officer, and that I had thrown away my uniform and put on civilian clothes to escape being captured by the Soviet occupation forces. I was locked up in a pigsty and was searched and interrogated almost nonstop for three days until my captors finally decided that they would not be able to extract any information from me and that they might as well let me go.

I remained in Kletzk until the middle of October. There would have been no way for me to leave sooner even if I had wanted to do so, because the NKVD—the Russian Secret Police—and militiamen recruited from among local Communist sympathizers had virtually sealed off the town. They patrolled the streets day and night, giving special attention to the railroad station and the highways that led out of Kletzk. The militiamen wore civilian clothes and were identified only by their red armbands, but some of them carried rifles. They were on the lookout for Polish soldiers, whom the Soviets regarded as Fascist enemies.

I looked for work, not only to earn money for food but also to keep my mind occupied, for my days and nights were filled with anxiety about my wife and our parents in Warsaw.

I found it impossible to get work in Kletzk. The town's so-called "capitalists," including the owners of little grocery stores who had struggled for a bare living ever since they could remember, had been arrested, and their stores had been confiscated. A low-type element, individuals who lived only from theft and blackmail, had taken power under the new Soviet order.

There were a number of Jews still in Kletzk, and I became acquainted with one Jewish family. Soon I was taking all my meals with them and, in fact, was spending most of my time at their home. One day they suggested that I should leave the barn where I had been living since my arrival on Rosh HaShanah and move in with them until I would be able to decide whether or not to remain in Kletzk. I happily accepted their invitation, hoping that someday I would be able to repay their kindness, if not directly to them, then at least by coming to the rescue of others in need of help.

In mid-October I learned that Warsaw had fallen to the Germans. Now I was convinced that my place was not in Kletzk but with my wife and our parents in Warsaw, either to protect them or to share whatever fate would have in store for them. I actively began to look for ways of leaving the Russian sector and returning to Nazi-occupied Warsaw.

By this time there were no more restrictions on travel from one town to another within the Soviet sector. But how was I to cross from the Soviet sector into the part of Poland which had been occupied by the Germans? I had heard that the border between the two sectors had been formalized and that the Soviets were patrolling their side of the frontier with great efficiency.

Hitler and Stalin had divided Poland between themselves on either side of a natural border—the River Bug.

In order to enter the German sector, I would have to cross that river.

I bade farewell to my friends in Kletzk and hitchhiked to the border, mostly in horse-drawn wagons. I discovered a peasant whose farm was almost at the edge of the river and who was familiar with the area on both banks. In return for my wrist watch, he agreed to ferry me across the river in his rowboat and to give me a loaf of bread.

We crossed the River Bug during the night of October 17. Once across, I had to make my way through densely wooded terrain and then waded in water up to my knees. Luckily, I did not encounter any border patrols, Russian or German.

My first stop in the German sector was a little forest from where a road led to a village. There, the peasant had told me, I would be able to obtain directions for the next stage of my journey to Warsaw. In the forest, I was abruptly stopped by a shout in German, "Halt! Who goes there?" My heart almost froze inside me. It was a German border patrolman, with his machine gun pointed straight at me. But I did not lose my nerve. With my blond hair, blue eyes and light complexion, and my perfect Polish which bore no trace of a Yiddish accent, I could easily pass for a Polish "Aryan."

I therefore told the German, in Polish, that I was a Pole from the west bank of the River Bug and had somehow strayed into the Soviet sector. He eyed me with suspicion, but luckily for me, he did not seem to be taking his duties too seriously. He asked me a few perfunctory questions, mostly about Russia and the Russians. I told him what he obviously wanted to hear: that I hated the Communists and that I preferred Hitler to Stalin any day. Finally, the German mumbled something under his breath. I could not make out what he was saying, but the idea was that I could pass. He did not even attempt to search me—again a lucky thing for me, for I still had my gun.

I was now "safe" inside the sector of Poland that had fallen to Hitler. I was exhausted. My foot still hurt, but I forced myself to keep going, half-limping, half-running, until I came to a railroad depot. I asked the stationmaster when the next train would be leaving for Warsaw. Aside from my gun, which I carried hidden beneath my shirt, my only "baggage" was the loaf of bread from the peasant at the border. I had not taken even a bite from the bread; I wanted to save it until I could share it with my family in Warsaw.

4

I arrived in Warsaw early in the morning of October 20, 1939, after an absence of six weeks. As I emerged from the station into the street I shuddered with disbelief. Though I had been born and raised in Warsaw, I could hardly recognize the city. The streets were piled high with rubble through which German soldiers cautiously picked their way. I moved as quickly as I could, eager to reach our apartment house, yet dreading what I might find there.

At last I turned the corner of the street where we lived. Our apartment building was still there. A miracle, I thought. I passed through the gateway and into the courtyard. The first person I met was Stanislaw, our janitor. When he saw me, his eyes grew wide with amazement. "Stanislaw!" I shouted breathlessly. "Is everybody all right?"

"Oh, yes, everybody is all right," Stanislaw replied slowly. "Except your mother. She is dead."

I dropped my loaf of bread which I had been carrying under my arm and raced up the six flights of steps to our

1938: My parents, Miriam and Max Starkopf, and I.

My mother-in-law, Miriam Miller

third-floor apartment. I pounded on the door with such force that I bruised my knuckles.

Moments later, the apartment door opened, ever so slightly. Looking out from the crack in the door was Pela, her face white with fear.

I rushed past her into the apartment and flung myself into the nearest chair. "What happened to Mother?" I cried. "If only I hadn't left..." I was sure that if only I had stayed with my family in Warsaw, my mother would still be alive.

My father came tottering into the room from the back of the apartment. During the six weeks I had been away, he seemed to have aged twenty years. His face was pale and his eyes were red and swollen. My heart bled for him.

After seconds of disbelief, my father and Pela flung themselves upon me, weeping, clinging to me, their hands stroking me timidly as if to make sure that I was really there and not a mirage. When at last we were able to speak, my father and Pela told me how my mother had died.

They began the story with the moment on September 6 when my mother and Pela had parted from me at the Kierbedz Bridge. As my mother led her away from the bridge, it had occurred to Pela that her only brother Ben, who had just turned 20, might also leave Warsaw to join the fighting forces and that she wanted to see him before he went.

When Pela and my mother returned to our apartment, my mother, who had kept her composure until then, collapsed in a dead faint. When she regained consciousness she began to weep and could not stop.

While my father tried to comfort my mother, Pela ran to her parents' house, only a few blocks away, to find out whether Ben was still there. Ben was six feet tall, unusually handsome and highly intelligent. He had studied German, French, Latin and Hebrew. Pela's family had been more religious than my own, and Ben himself had been an ardent Zionist. Before the war he had organized two Zionist youth groups in Warsaw. He had been ready to go to Palestine himself when the outbreak of the war put a stop to his plans.

At her parents' apartment Pela learned that Ben was still asleep. He had spent all night on trench-digging duty. Had they not heard the radio instructions that all young men were to leave Warsaw and report in Brzesc for mobilization? Pela inquired. No, her parents replied; their radio was not working. Ben awoke, and Pela told him about the mobilization orders. Still under the impact of my departure, she urged her brother to go to Brzesc also. "You don't want to be pointed out as a draft evader, do you?" she demanded.

Hearing this, my mother-in-law burst into hysterical weeping. She begged Ben not to leave, but Ben would not listen to her. Flushed with patriotic enthusiasm, he threatened to leave without saying good-by if his mother would not stop crying.

When my mother-in-law understood at last that Ben was determined to go, she rummaged for his hiking knapsack and began to stuff it with clothing. She was so confused that she put in her own clothes instead of her son's. Pela gently pushed her mother aside. "You leave the packing to me, Mama," she said.

Pela and her parents accompanied Ben out of the apartment building and into the street. Then Pela suddenly realized that she had forgotten to put food into Ben's knapsack. So she rushed over to our apartment for some canned meat and vegetables and a loaf of bread. She also brought out a "tea egg," with a handle like a spoon, which could be filled with enough tea leaves for

32

brewing one cup of tea. I mention this tea egg because it was to turn up again later on.

My mother-in-law took off her gold wedding ring and slipped it onto Ben's finger. "If you're ever hungry," she said to him, "you can exchange this ring for a piece of bread."

In the apartment building where Pela and I lived with my parents, there also lived, on the second floor, a family by the name of Gingold. Before the war, Mr. Gingold had been the manager of one of Warsaw's largest shirt factories. The Gingolds had two children—a son of 18 and a daughter of 12. The son, Martin, had just graduated gymnasium and his father, unlike Pela's parents and mine, believed that the countryside would be a safer place for young people than Warsaw. The Gingolds were therefore not only willing but in fact anxious that Martin should leave the city. So, when Mr. Gingold saw Pela hurrying down the steps with the food and the "tea egg" and learned that Ben was about to leave, he eagerly suggested that Martin should go with him. "Never mind Brzesc," said Mr. Gingold, "as long as he's away from Warsaw and all the bombs."

After the two young men had left, the Gingolds and my parents-in-law wept, but Pela actually felt relieved. She was certain she had done the right thing in urging Ben to leave Warsaw because the streets were filled with men, women and children, some in cars, some on bicycles and some on foot, laden with their belongings, in a frantic rush to flee from the city before the Germans moved in.

Warsaw was bombed day and night. The city had been caught unprepared. No air raid shelters had been set up. People took cover in cellars. Before the war, these cellars had served as storage places for sacks of potatoes, bins of coal and stacks of firewood. Now they had become temporary homes for whole families, complete with tables, chairs and cots.

Most of Warsaw's grocery stores had sold out their stock and had closed down, but people still formed endless lines in front of bakeries, waiting all day and all night for a loaf of bread, refusing to take shelter even when the air-raid sirens went off. The citizens of Warsaw seemed to be less afraid of bombs than of starving to death.

Pela was then working in the office of a cannery. She insisted on reporting for work every morning even though she and the other employees had to spend most of the day in the emergency shelter that had been set up in the basement of the plant. My mother begged Pela not to go to work. The basement might be safe, she argued, but what if Pela were caught in an air raid while she was in the street, on the way to or from work? But my wife, who has always had a well-developed sense of responsibility, insisted that as long as people were in need of food and the cannery continued to operate, it was her duty to report at the office. Before the war, she had been a book-keeper. Now her job was to sell canned foods to civilians and to the supply officers of the Polish armed forces. Each morning when Pela arrived at the plant, the police had to run interference for her through the crowds that blocked the entrance, waiting for the plant to open so they could buy food.

On Friday morning, September 15—the day the Dolniaks and I arrived in Brzesc—Pela returned from work to find her parents in our apartment. Their own apartment building had been damaged by bombs so that they had no longer felt it safe to remain there.

It was the eve of Rosh HaShanah, the Jewish New Year. In honor of the holiday my mother had obtained two chicken wings and had put them up in a kettle of water for soup. However, she could not finish the cooking because the air raid sirens started up again and everyone in the building rushed to the basement. Evening came and it was time for the service which traditionally ushers in the holiday, but of course no one could go to the synagogue because the bombing had not stopped. My parents, Pela's parents and the other Jewish tenants of our apartment building decided to hold the service right there in the basement. Pela told me how the men sang the ancient chants of the High Holiday prayer book, while the young mothers hugged their children in their arms and wailed in Polish and Yiddish, "Dear God in Heaven! Have mercy! Don't punish our children for our sins! Save them! Let them survive this horror!"

On the next day, September 16, the first day of Rosh HaShanah, Pela stayed home from work not only because of the holiday but also because the ceaseless bombing made it virtually impossible for anyone to venture out into the street, or even to leave the basement shelters.

Towards evening there seemed to be a lull in the bombing. Pela and our parents went upstairs to my parents' apartment to heat some food for a quick supper. As they sat down at the table, my mother suddenly said, "I don't feel well," and fainted. Pela and my father attempted to revive her. She opened her eyes for a moment, murmured, "Adam! Adam! My boy!" and then she lost consciousness again.

My mother-in-law rushed out into the street to fetch the doctor who lived half a block away. The falling debris made the streets unsafe; besides, the curfew had gone into effect and anyone caught outdoors during curfew hours could be summarily shot. But Pela's mother was not afraid of any danger to herself as long as she was doing what had to be done.

At first the doctor refused to go with her. There was no point in risking his own life, he protested, when the patient herself was probably beyond help, anyway. But Pela's mother went down on her knees, kissed his hands and begged him to have mercy. This apparently moved the doctor, because he finally agreed to accompany her to our apartment. But by the time he and my mother-in-law arrived there, it was too late. While I lay in the barn in Kletzk, hundreds of miles away, my mother had died in Pela's arms. The last word she said had been my name.

Two days later—on the day after Rosh HaShanah—my mother was buried in Warsaw's Jewish cemetery. Due to the bombing and because anti-aircraft defenses had been set up in the Jewish cemetery, most of the Jews who died during those days of siege were buried by their families, quickly and unceremoniously, in the courtyards or backyards of their apartment buildings. But Pela's mother insisted that a woman like my mother deserved a proper burial. Therefore, despite the danger, my father agreed to a traditional funeral in the Jewish cemetery. In years to come, Pela was to remember my mother's funeral as one of the most harrowing experiences of her life.

Somehow, after seemingly endless searching and bargaining, my father was able to hire a horse-drawn wagon. He himself gently pushed the wooden casket with my mother's body onto the wagon. But at this point the driver of the wagon balked and refused to budge from our street. He was not going to have his horse killed and his wagon blown up in an air raid, he said, just because somebody was crazy enough to insist on holding a regular funeral at a time like this. In the end my father mounted the driver's seat and drove the wagon to the cemetery himself. Pela and her parents followed on foot. My mother's two sisters, who lived near us, were told that my mother had died, but they were afraid to venture out of their homes, let alone go to the cemetery where the anti-aircraft guns were in constant action.

36

The Jewish cemetery was only about a mile and a half from our apartment building, but it took the cortege several hours to get there. The horse, a starved bag of skin and bones, turned skittish from the whistling of the bombs and the thunder of the anti-aircraft fire. Finally, my father had to get off the wagon and lead the horse by its reins.

Passing a bombed-out building on Okopowa Street, which ran parallel to the cemetery, Pela saw a woman's head lolling from a pile of crushed bricks in an upper story. It was, she remembered, a very beautiful young face with long, blond hair. The eyes were wide open and it seemed to Pela that they were staring directly at her. Pela stumbled and almost fell but her mother held her firmly. "My child," she said to my wife, "you must keep calm. You must not lose control of yourself. You are performing an act of loving kindness, giving your husband's mother the last honor she deserves so that she will rest in a proper Jewish grave. You will see—God will reward you for this by letting you live to see your husband again."

Every few minutes the mourners had to stop and duck into a building, or a cellar, for shelter from the bombs. My father told me that he himself did not care whether he lived or died, but the Polish civil defense patrols were out in full force and would not permit anyone in the streets while the bombs fell. It was, my father said, a sheer miracle that they reached the cemetery alive and with the wagon and the coffin intact.

In the cemetery, Pela's father, who had studied at a Jewish religious school, hurriedly recited the burial service. His words were almost drowned out by the deafening noise of the bombs and the anti-aircraft fire.

Now, a month later, my father attempted to comfort me. I must not feel that my leaving home had caused my mother's death, he said. If anyone was to blame, he told me, it was those neighbors who had left Warsaw with me but had turned back the very first night. They had told everyone they met in Warsaw that the journey to Brzesc would be a "death march," and that they were sure I could not possibly survive it. In fact, they declared, I might very well be dead already. Someone passed the word to my mother, who did not want to alarm Pela but shared her fears with my father. "If Adam is no longer alive," she had said, "I don't want to live anymore either." Certain that I had died, my mother had, as it were, willed her own death.

The day after my mother's funeral, Pela went back to work at the cannery, braving the bombs and the gunfire each day in order to help serve the soldiers and civilians who needed the food.

Three days before Warsaw surrendered to the Germans, the cannery where Pela worked was taken over by the Polish army. Only then did Pela decide that it was more important for her to stay at home to look after her own parents and my grieving father.

On Tuesday, September 26, the mayor of Warsaw, Stefan Starzynski, announced over the radio that, in order to prevent further loss of life, he had declared Warsaw an open city. He explained that he had done his best to defend Warsaw against the German invaders but that the armed forces available to him had been no match for the enemy's superior personnel and equipment.

The next day Warsaw was bombed around the clock. There was no longer any water, gas or electricity. The State Radio went off the air. The basements, pitch dark because of the shortage of candles, were crowded with starved Polish soldiers who had deserted from the army and were mingling freely with the panic-stricken civilians. Soldiers and civilians joined in looting those few grocery stores that were still open for business. Soldiers knocked at apartment doors, begging for old civilian clothes into which they could change so they would not be seized by the Germans as prisoners of war.

On September 29, 1939, exactly four weeks after the outbreak of the war in Poland, the German army occupied Warsaw. At first, as they rolled into the city in long columns of army trucks, the German soldiers threw loaves of bread into the streets, "for the hungry Poles," as they put it. But whenever they saw someone who looked to them like a Jew bending to pick up a loaf of bread, they would push him away with their rifle butts. As the civilians scrambled for the bread, German army photographers took movies which were sent back to the "home front" to show how generous the German conquerors were with their enemies, the Poles.

German troops occupied the newly-built Warsaw Court House on Leszno and Ogrodowa Streets and several buildings on Novolipki Street, where our apartment building was located. Fortunately for us, they stopped two blocks away from our building. The apartment buildings which the Germans had selected for occupation were still in fairly good condition. Most of the tenants were Jews. The Germans, Pela told me, gave the Jews about five minutes to leave and stood there with pocket watches in their hands. Any Jews still inside the buildings after the deadline were shot and later dumped into mass graves.

Pela and my father wanted to be prepared to leave our apartment at a moment's notice. Pela therefore packed the most necessary things for herself and my father into one suitcase. Pela's parents by then had gone back to their own apartment. Their window panes had been blown out but they found the apartment still habitable.

But most important, the building had been damaged by bombs and hence, my mother-in-law insisted, would probably be spared occupation by the Germans.

On October 4, 1939, the Gestapo in Warsaw appointed a *Judenrat*—the term is best translated as "Jew Council" (nothing so dignified as "Jewish Council")—consisting of twenty-four hand-picked members of the Jewish community. The chairman of the *Judenrat* was a civil engineer named Adam Czerniakow. The function of the *Judenrat* in Warsaw—as with similar organizations which the Germans were to set up in other cities—was to carry out the orders of the Gestapo. In the case of Warsaw, the *Judenrat*'s first assignment was to take a census of Warsaw's Jewish population, which was then approximately 400,000. All Jews were ordered to wear white armbands with a blue Star of David. These armbands were to be worn on the right arm. Jews caught in the street without their armbands were arrested, imprisoned and in some cases summarily shot. Before long, the lobbies of apartment houses with Jewish tenants (the ghetto had not yet been established) were plastered with signs reading, "Where is your armband? Do not leave your home without it."

Gradually, men of military age who had left Warsaw during the siege straggled back into the city. Among the returnees was Pela's uncle Ludek, who had joined the Polish army on the first day of the war. When he entered his store, his wife Helena and their teenage son Mundek, who had kept the store going during his absence, did not recognize him. "Give that beggar some money," Helena said to Mundek. When Ludek did not extend his hand to take the money but remained standing in silence, looking at his wife and son, Helena said to him, "Isn't there anything I can do for you?" Only when Ludek burst into tears did Helena finally understand that this unshaven tattered creature was her husband.

The two older Gold brothers returned. Rysio, the youngest, had been killed by the Germans. The editor Kaplan, and his son, "Jerzyk II," were also dead. Jerzyk and Lutek Gold broke the news to Mrs. Kaplan, then went to Pela and told her that no doubt I, too, had been killed. Mrs. Kaplan apparently lost her will to live, for she became ill and died soon afterwards. Pela and my father never discussed the possibility that I might be dead. Pela had never reported to him what the Gold brothers had told her, and my father had never mentioned to Pela what my mother had said to him before she died. But both Pela and my father, each of them alone, had resigned themselves to the thought that they would never see me again. And so, when they heard my frantic knocks on the apartment door, they could think of nothing else but that the Germans had finally come for them.

Now the three of us—Pela, my father and I—sat huddled together on the living room sofa, crying and kissing and caressing each other ever so often, still not believing that we were together again.

In the end, it was I who broke our embrace. I wanted to wash, shave and change my clothes. I wanted to look and feel like a human being again. Meanwhile, my father had regained his composure. He went to Pela's parents to tell them the good news and brought them back with him to our apartment. Then all the five of us went to the cemetery to visit my mother's grave, which was identified only by a crude wooden marker. We stood there for a long time. I had one arm around Pela, the other around my father, but I was the only one who wept. It seemed that Pela and my father, who had been with my mother when she died, had no tears left. The thought came to me that perhaps God had been good to my mother; He had taken her before she could have fallen into the hands of the Germans.

5

Pela's parents accompanied us from the cemetery back to our apartment. My mother-in-law plied me with questions about her only son, Pela's brother Ben, who had left Warsaw with our neighbor Martin Gingold on the same day as I. Had I, by any chance, met Ben anywhere? Had I heard any news about him? It took me hours to convince her that I had neither seen Ben nor heard anything about him. When at last she understood that I knew nothing about her son she collapsed in tears. It took my father-in-law a long time to calm her down sufficiently for him to take her home.

I rested at home for about a week. But as the days passed, I became increasingly unhappy with my mother-in-law's mental and emotional state. I saw that Pela, too, was terribly upset. She had begun to feel that her mother was angry at her for having urged Ben to leave Warsaw. She was convinced that her mother would never forgive her if anything had happened to Ben.

Fearing that not only my mother-in-law but also Pela would break down under the strain I decided on a desperate act. I would leave Warsaw again and return to the Russian sector to find Ben. This time I would not travel by myself but would take Pela with me. We would not take my father or Pela's parents with us because we felt it would be madness to put these three elderly people through the dangers of flight from the German sector. Our plan was to stay temporarily in some city or larger town in the Russian sector and from there start a search for Ben. If we located him we would get hold of him and bring him back with us to Warsaw. Life in the Russian sector, we reasoned, had its own uncertainties; if Ben was still alive, at least let him be together with the rest of us again.

Naturally, we informed the Gingolds of our plan. They suggested that we head for Rovno, 250 miles east of Warsaw, where they had relatives. When their son Martin left Warsaw with Ben, Mr. Gingold had advised the young men to try to contact these relatives and, if possible, to visit them. Mr. Gingold gave me the address of his relatives. Rovno was now in the Russian sector. Perhaps the Gingold cousins would know what had become of Ben and Martin.

At the last moment, we decided to reveal our project also to our very close friends, Moniek and Donia Bronstern. Moniek had gone to school with me. His wife, Donra, had been Pela's schoolmate, and I had been best man at their wedding. Moniek was a physician. Because of the Jewish quota at the Polish universities, Moniek, like many other young Polish Jews who had wanted to study medicine during the 1930's, had gone to Italy. He had received his doctorate in medicine from the University of Pisa and had returned to Warsaw shortly before the outbreak of the war. The Bronsterns listened to our story first with incredulity, then with growing interest. The next morning they came to our apartment and told us that they wanted to go with us to Rovno. Perhaps they would be able to help us find Ben. But instead of returning to Warsaw with us, they would remain in the Russian sector and register as refugees. Since doctors were always in demand, Donia said, Moniek should be able to establish a practice or find a position in a hospital somewhere in the Russian sector.

By this time "border smuggling" between the German and Russian sectors of Poland had been developed into quite a lucrative business by individuals, mostly peasants, who lived near the boundary between the two sectors and who were familiar with the terrain on both sides. In return for exorbitant fees, payable in cash, jewelry or other scarce articles, these peasants would guide Jews from the German sector into the Russian-occupied area. At this early stage the Russian border patrols for the most part tacitly agreed to look the other way when Jews entered their territory from the German side. The danger came from the Germans; if German border patrols caught a Jew near the frontier, they would rob him of everything he had before permitting him to pass them. In many instances, it was the peasant "border guides" who did the robbing. Not satisfied with the payment offered by the unfortunate Jew, they would virtually strip him naked before depositing him in no-man's land, from where, if he still had any strength left, he could then make his way into the Russian sector.

The four of us—the Bronsterns, Pela and I—experienced such a hold-up ourselves. After traveling by train to a point not too far from the border, we hired a horse and wagon to take us to a border village. In that village we located a peasant who agreed to smuggle us into the Russian sector for a cash fee which seemed reasonable to us. At about 7 o'clock that evening we set out from the village on foot, accompanied by our peasant guide. It was dark and the highway was deserted. Suddenly, shadows materialized from the darkness.

"Hand over everything you have!" a voice said in Polish. In an instant, three or four men were upon us. Luckily, I still had with me the gun I had picked up from the highway to Brzesc. The mere feel of my weapon under my belt gave me courage. Moniek and I began to shout ferociously in Polish and to strike out with our fists in every direction. Again good fortune was with us: our attackers, apparently Polish rowdies from the village, fled. So did our peasant.

We hid in the woods near the village until midnight. Then we crossed the border, without trouble and without the benefit of a guide.

After we were well inside the Russian sector, we looked for the nearest railway depot. At the depot, we learned that there was no direct train from this locality to Rovno. The nearest large city was Brzesc, 150 miles north of Rovno. When I had left Brzesc by ambulance, I had been sure that the city would be occupied by the Germans, but now I was told that Brzesc, like Rovno, was in the hands of the Russians.

We boarded the next train to Brzesc. Perhaps, I said, we would be able to locate the friends whom Pela and I had made there before the war. If we found them, we would leave Pela with them while the Bronsteins and I would go on to Rovno—Moniek to investigate employment possibilities and I to contact the relatives of Mr. Gingold. Pela was close to exhaustion and I wanted to keep her, if at all possible, from hearing bad news about her brother at first hand.

Brzesc seemed to have made a surprisingly good recovery from the savage bombings of the month before. Stores had reopened and the streets, fairly clear of rubble, were busy again. To my pleasant surprise, I found our friends, still living in their apartment building. They were thin and tired, but they were delighted to see us and agreed at once to have Pela stay with them while the Bronsterns and I were in Rovno.

Very early the next morning, the Bronsterns and I went back to the station and bought tickets for the next train to Rovno. We were told that we would have to change trains in Kovel, about midway on the journey, and that we would have a six-hour wait between trains, from 11 in the morning until 5 in the afternoon.

Moniek said he would use the opportunity to see what hospital or other health facility there was in Kovel and to inquire where refugee physicians could register for employment. I agreed to accompany him and Donia into the town.

In Kovel we hired a horse and carriage for the short ride from the station to the town's small hospital. Moniek and Donia went inside; I did not care to go in and waited for them in the street. I could not have known then that I would regret this decision before the day was out.

It did not take Moniek long to make his inquiries and we were back at the station with plenty of time to spare until the train for Rovno was due.

We arrived at Rovno at nine o'clock that evening and took a horse-drawn cab to the apartment of the Gingold relatives.

To my amazement, we were greeted at the door by Martin Gingold. He was so surprised to see us that it took him some moments to recover his speech and invite the Bronsterns and me to come inside.

Yes, he told me, he knew where Ben was. He had made the entire journey from Warsaw to Rovno on foot, but he had had to leave Ben at a hospital on the way because Ben had become very ill. It was typhoid fever, the doctors had said, but Ben was in no immediate danger. Martin had gone on to Rovno alone, found his cousins and had moved in with them. Only a few days ago, he said, he had made the trip to visit Ben at the hospital and had found him much improved. Ben seemed to have passed the crisis and was well on the way to recovery. The hospital, Martin told us, was in Kovel.

I shook my head in disbelief. Only hours before, I had waited for Moniek and Donia in front of that hospital, unwilling to accompany them inside. If only I had known then that Ben was there! I wanted to return to Kovel at once. Martin offered to go with me.

46

As we traveled to Kovel on the night train, Martin told me how kind Ben had been to him during their flight from Warsaw. His eyes filled with tears as he recalled how, spent with hunger, they had found a large turnip on the highway and Ben had taken only one small bite, insisting that Martin eat the rest.

We arrived in Kovel at seven o'clock in the morning and took a horse and carriage straight to the hospital, promising the driver a double fare if he would only make his horse go fast. Despite Martin's encouraging report I had an uneasy feeling about what I would find in Kovel.

At the hospital I asked for the resident doctor, introduced myself as Ben's brother-in-law and said I wanted to see Ben.

The doctor shook his head, gave me a sad look and informed me that Ben had died only half an hour earlier. He had passed the crisis but apparently his heart had failed.

I felt as if my legs had turned into jelly, but I did not fall. I asked the doctor to let me see Ben's body. Perhaps there had been a mistake. Hospitals were so overcrowded now; it would be very easy to make an error in identifying a patient.

Without a word, the doctor took Martin and me to the basement where an improvised morgue had been set up. He uncovered one of the bodies. Even in my state of shock I could see that this was Ben. I touched his face; it was still warm. I cried like an infant. If only I had known yesterday that Ben was in the hospital, perhaps I could have saved him! With my own strength and energy, I felt, I could have willed him to live. Or at least I could have been at his side so that he would not have died alone.

Something inside me still refused to accept Ben's death. I asked the doctor to have the patient's personal effects brought to me. An attendant brought in Ben's tattered clothes, his wrist watch, the gold wedding ring which his mother had slipped onto his finger, and the "tea egg" which Pela had slid into his knapsack at the last moment before he and Martin Gingold had left Warsaw. There could be no doubt now; the skeleton that lay before me on a slab in the morgue was Ben.

How was I going to break the news to Pela in Brzesc and to her parents back in Warsaw? Almost at once I decided that I would not tell them at all. Everyone had to keep his nerves strong in order to survive. Under the circumstances Pela and her parents should not be forced to confront the certainty that Ben was dead. Much better to let them cling indefinitely to the hope that Ben was still alive somewhere. In time, very gradually, I felt, they might come to the conclusion themselves that they would never see Ben again, but I would not be the one to deal them that final blow.

Martin and I were now faced with the task of making funeral arrangements for Ben. He would have to be buried immediately, right there in Kovel. I sold my mother-in-law's wedding ring to give Ben a decent burial. I did not want to use the last of the money I had brought along with me on the journey from Warsaw, for if I returned to Brzesc without money Pela would suspect at once that something had gone very wrong.

Because Pela's family observed the main tenets of our religion, I arranged for a funeral that would be in keeping with strict Orthodox Jewish tradition. I had the body wrapped in a plain white sheet and bought a plain pine box as a casket. Then I paid a peasant to take the body in his wagon to the town's Jewish cemetery. Martin and I followed on foot. In the cemetery I even managed to find a *tehillim-zoger*, a "psalm chanter" who earned a few zlotys here and there by reciting graveside prayers. I paid him to chant the burial service. Then I, as the only

48

member of Ben's family present, recited the Mourners' Kaddish.

As I watched the gravediggers fill up the open grave with earth I could not help recalling that only a month earlier Pela had accompanied my mother on her last journey while I was far away and did not even know that my mother had died. Now positions had been reversed; I was burying Pela's brother while Pela was waiting for me in Brzesc, unaware of his death.

However, this was no time for philosophizing. It was much more important to console Martin Gingold, who was standing beside me before the grave, shaking with sobs.

Martin and I took the next train back to Rovno, where we broke the news to Martin's relatives and to the Bronsterns. I wanted desperately to be with Pela in Brzesc, but I knew that if I returned so soon Pela would question me why I had given up the search for her brother so abruptly.

Martin and I concocted a story designed to bolster Pela's hopes that Ben was still alive. To corroborate the tale I planned to tell Pela, I wrote out a letter which I asked Martin to copy, in his own handwriting, with not one word altered. He was to sign this letter with his name and mail it to me in Brzesc, in care of the friends with whom Pela had been staying, a few days after my own departure from Rovno. It was to be a letter from Martin, addressed to me, telling me how sorry he was that he had missed my visit; when I arrived in Rovno, he had been out of town. He was sure, however, that his relatives had told me everything he himself knew about Ben. He and Ben had attempted to cross the Polish border into neutral Rumania, from where they had hoped to reach Palestine by way of the Black Sea, as so many other Jews from Poland had done successfully since the outbreak of the war. However, Martin and Ben had been stopped at the border and he, Martin, had been turned back by the border patrol. But he had seen Ben slip through and while he, Martin, would probably have to remain in Rovno until the end of the war, Ben by now undoubtedly had arrived in Palestine, where he had always wanted to go.

Martin and I agreed that Pela and even her parents would believe our story. Since there were no postal communications between Poland and Palestine, they naturally would not expect to receive a letter directly from Ben until after the war.

Leaving the letter for Martin to copy, I bade farewell to him and the Bronsteins and went back to Brzesc. Of course, Pela was surprised to see me again so soon. But I put on a cheerful smile and told her the encouraging news which Martin's relatives had given me about Ben. To prove to Pela that I had really seen Martin's relatives, and that Martin had indeed managed to get to Rovno, I handed her the "tea egg" which she had given to Ben in Warsaw and which had been handed to me at the hospital in Kovel with the rest of Ben's personal possessions.

Several days later, Martin's letter arrived in Brzesc. He had faithfully copied the text I had left with him, adding only that he would try to come to Brzesc himself within the next few days to visit Pela and me.

It did not occur to Pela to question my story then. We had known each other ever since I had been thirteen and she twelve, and in all those years we had never had a secret from one another. This would be the first time I had ever lied to her, but I felt that this would be far kinder than to tell her the truth about Ben now.

Pela saw no reason to wait in Brzesc for Martin Gingold. She insisted that we return to Warsaw as soon as possible to share the good news with her parents. But by this time I had second thoughts about leaving the Russian sector and walking back into the Nazi trap. My old independence and cool logic had reasserted themselves and I said to Pela that it would be insane for both of us to return to the German sector now. I had changed my mind about allowing my father and Pela's parents to remain in Warsaw. I now felt that the strain, and even the risks, to which they might be put in a flight from Nazi-occupied Warsaw into the Russian sector would be much less dangerous for them than the constant peril to which they would be exposed if they continued to live under the guns of Hitler's Gestapo.

We discussed the situation with our friends in Brzesc, and they, too, strongly urged us to have our parents join us in the Russian zone. They suggested that Pela should return to Warsaw without me, persuade my father and her own parents to leave everything and then bring them with her to me in Brzesc. Pela would not have to cross into the German sector by herself. A young woman whom Pela knew and who was now living in Brzesc also had relatives in Warsaw. She had been waiting for an opportunity to go there and rescue them. She was young and strong and felt she would never be able to forgive herself if she remained safe in Brzesc and abandoned her relatives in Warsaw to their fate.

Pela's friends made contact with a peasant who lived on the Russian side of the border and who had been recommended to them as an honest, trustworthy individual. It was agreed that he would not only escort Pela and the young woman across the border but would accompany them to Warsaw and then bring them back to Brzesc along with our parents.

I accompanied Pela and the young woman to the village from which they were to cross the border. There, we parted and I moved in with the peasant's family to wait there until Pela's return.

Ten days later the peasant returned—alone. Faithful to his promise, he had accompanied Pela and her friend all the way to Warsaw and then escorted them back to the border crossing point nearest his village. But now, he told me, the two women were stuck in no-man's land because the Russian border patrols at this crossing point had suddenly received strict orders to watch out for "illegals"—meaning, of course, Jews—who would attempt to cross into the Russian sector. So, the peasant said, Pela and her friend were only two miles away from his cottage but were unable to pass the Russian border patrols. He, the peasant, had been permitted to cross only because he carried papers certifying that he was not a refugee but a permanent resident in the Russian sector.

I decided to set out at once to find Pela. In order not to look conspicuous, I put on some work clothes that belonged to the peasant. Then, together with the peasant, I marched off to the place where he said Pela would be.

When we arrived in a broad open space which now belonged neither to Germany nor to Russia, I stopped in amazement. The dark, clear December sky was red with the flames of dozens of campfires. Huddled around the campfires were refugees—hundreds and hundreds of them—and they all were chanting something in a discordant chorus, over and over again. At first I could not make out what they were chanting, but as I came closer, I could hear the words quite plainly: "Let us in! Let us in! You can shoot us, but don't turn us back! Better dead than living under the Germans!"

Fortunately, as it turned out, the Russian border patrols had orders not to shoot at the refugees. As a result, they were unable to hold them back for long and finally permitted them, in small groups, to pass into the Russian sector.

As the long lines of men, women and children moved past the place where I was standing, I frantically looked for Pela and her friend. When I saw them at last and Pela was in my arms, I was still so bewildered by the whole spectacle that I did not even ask Pela why her parents and my father were not with her.

I spoke a few words of Russian; so I approached one of the Russian border patrolmen who looked as if he outranked the others, and asked him to give the three of us a safe-conduct pass so that we would not be turned back at some other point. The officer was a decent fellow; he actually ordered one of his men to escort us into the Russian sector. It seemed that while, officially, the Russians were acceding to the demands of the Germans not to admit any more Jews into the Russian sector, they were sorry for the Jewish refugees and helped them whenever that was possible.

After we had arrived at the peasant's cottage, Pela told me why she had returned without my father and her own parents. With the help of Martin Gingold's letter, she had been able to convince her parents that Ben must be safe, but she had been unable to persuade either her parents or my father to leave Warsaw and return with her to the Russian sector. Only a little over two months had passed since Warsaw's surrender to the Germans. Already, the Germans had imposed restrictions upon the Jews in Warsaw, but there was still no ghetto and Jews were still largely permitted to live and work where they chose. As a result, many Jews, especially the older ones, now believed that it would be possible for them to exist in Warsaw even under German occupation, and that at any rate nothing would be gained at this point by leaving everything one owned and making the perilous crossing into the unknown. Most of the Jews of our parents' age did not take kindly to the idea of becoming penniless, unwanted refugees under the Russians, whom they viewed with suspicion. My father and Pela's parents had even tried to talk Pela into remaining with them in Warsaw and sending the peasant back to Brzesc alone with a message to me that I was to go back with him to Warsaw.

Difficult though it was, Pela did not listen to our parents. She told my parents that she would go back to Brzesc herself and bring me back to Warsaw. She said she did not trust the peasant to carry out this new mission alone. Then, with a heavy heart, she bade farewell to her parents, met the peasant at the place where they had agreed to meet, and returned to the Russian sector.

Pela and I left the peasant's cottage and returned to her friends in Brzesc. When we arrived, our friends handed us a new letter from Martin Gingold. Martin had written this letter on his own initiative. Once again he promised to visit us in Brzesc at the earliest opportunity. And again, he repeated our story of Ben's escape into Rumania.

But when I gave Pela the letter to read she turned pale.

"What have you been trying to keep from me?" she demanded. "Something has happened to my brother Ben."

She pointed to place after place in the letter where Martin had written *brat*—the Polish word for "brother." Each time, it was spelled with a capital "B." In Polish, this is the customary way of referring to a relative who is no longer alive. The capital letter shows respect for the dead.

Pela insisted that Martin and I knew something had happened to Ben and that we had conspired to keep it from her and her parents. I could not calm her down. I was furious with Martin. The first letter he had sent to me had been copied by him from my own longhand draft and I, of course, had been careful to spell *brat* with a lower-case "b." But now, with his second letter, Martin had spoiled everything. I told myself that I must not be too hard on Martin. He was, after all, only a boy of 18 and he had gone through hell. One could hardly expect him to think of such details as making sure of his own accord that he would not spell *brat* with a capital "B."

Pela had worked herself into a frenzy of anger and anxiety. She threatened that if I did not tell her the truth, she would go to Rovno herself, visit Martin Gingold and his relatives, and demand the truth from them. I had no alternative now but to tell her that Ben was dead.

Of course Pela was grief-stricken. Ben had been her only brother and her family's darling. But my fears about Pela's reaction to Ben's death turned out to be exaggerated. She was terribly brave; it was as if she had prepared herself both mentally and emotionally for the eventuality that Ben had not survived. She wept in my arms for some time, but then she dried her eyes and asked me to take her to Kovel at once. "I want to see the grave," she said.

We made the trip to Kovel that same day. After leaving the cemetery we went directly to a stonecutter to order a simple marker for Ben's grave. The stonecutter gave us his word of honor that he would place the marker on the grave as soon as the snow and ice would melt from the ground, and that he would do it even if we were no longer in Kovel by that time. We paid him his fee and took the train back to Brzesc.

6

In Brzesc, Pela made it clear to me that, particularly in view of the fact that Ben would never come home again, we owed it to her parents and my father to return to Warsaw together and to remain with them. "Whatever will happen now, the family must not be separated," she said. I was unable to put up an effective argument against that point because I knew that she was right.

However, this was not an opportune time to cross the border back into the German sector. The snow had begun to fall in earnest. Also, the borders between the two sectors had become stabilized at most points and stringent orders had been issued to border patrols on both sides to keep the borders sealed. We decided to remain with our friends in Brzesc over Christmas, until the end of December, when, we hoped, the border patrols in both sectors would have settled down to a steady, comparatively relaxed winter routine and we would be able to make the crossing with at least a fair chance of not being caught on either side.

On December 30, 1939, Pela and I set out on our journey to the border. We carried almost nothing with us except for a bottle of vodka to drink or to rub on our hands and faces for protection against the cold. This time we were determined to cross the border without a guide, in an area which Pela's friends had mapped out to me in detail. We wore leather boots but the snow reached up to our knees. It was a ten-mile walk from the last village on the Russian side to the point where we planned to cross the border.

During the night from December 30 to December 31 we were able to cover only half of the ten miles, because of the bitter cold. I rubbed Pela's hands and face with vodka to protect her from frostbite but it brought her little relief. She begged me to leave her and go on alone. But of course both of us knew that this was out of the question. I carried her in my arms as far as I could. After a while I took off my heavy overcoat and left it in the snow so I would have less weight to carry.

Early the next morning we came upon an abandoned hut in the woods. It looked like the type of cottage in which forest rangers lived during the summer season but which was uninhabitable during the winter. The door

56

was unlocked; we went inside and stayed there all that day, waiting for nightfall to continue our journey.

At one point we had to climb over a railroad embankment. The embankment was covered with frozen snow so that we kept sliding down. Our hands were so stiff and numb with the cold that we could not grasp a rock or a tree trunk for support. But luck was with us once again. Early in the morning of January 1, 1940, we reached the railroad station of a town called Malkinia, well inside the German sector. There was a direct train linking Malkinia with Warsaw. Before long, Malkinia was to gain sad notoriety as the railroad junction at which hundreds of thousands of human beings would arrive by train from Warsaw, to be herded into other trains bound for a village called Treblinka. But all that was still in the future. When we arrived at the station on New Year's Day, 1940, there were no other passengers waiting there for a train.

We learned that the next train to Warsaw was due in Malkinia in two hours' time. The problem now was to find a warm shelter where we could spend those two hours thawing our bodies without the risk of being stopped and asked to show our papers. I was afraid that, looking as spent and bedraggled as we did, and as the only passengers waiting in the station on a holiday, we might attract the attention of a German official on the lookout for "illegals" or Jews.

We approached a railroad employee and asked him to take us to a place where we could warm up until the Warsaw train arrived. He led us to a railroad car which stood on a siding. This car, he explained, was reserved for men who worked on the tracks. The car was old, dirty and dank, but it was warm and therefore seemed like paradise to Pela and me. In the middle of the car was a cast-iron stove, its top red-hot from the coal fire inside.

Pela and I sat down on the floor in one corner of the car. We saw that there were a few other people in the car, too, but it was too dark inside for us to see their faces.

Suddenly I felt deathly sick. Perhaps it was from the vodka I had drunk to fortify myself and to keep warm for the border crossing. The heat and the stale smell in the railroad car had probably done the rest. At any rate, I rushed out of the car and was sick in the snow outside.

Afterwards, as I walked back toward the car, I saw two German soldiers standing in front of the car, talking with some Polish railroad workers. The Poles were telling them that the cold weather seemed to be keeping the Jews from attempting to cross into the Russian sector. To this, one of the German soldiers replied, in a broken Polish, "I wish I could get my hands on one of those damned Jewish swine." It was lucky that both Pela and I were blond-haired and blue-eyed so that either of us could have passed for prime examples of the "Aryan" super species. So I sauntered nonchalantly toward the car and even smiled at the Germans as I passed them and climbed aboard. When the Warsaw train pulled into the station, Pela and I boarded it without any trouble.

We arrived in Warsaw at 11 o'clock that morning and went directly to our apartment. My father was overjoyed to see us. He had never expected Pela, let alone me, to return to Warsaw. He made us sit down and rest while he rushed to tell Pela's parents that we had come. Within minutes, he was back with Pela's parents. Pela bravely stuck to the story that Ben was probably in Palestine by now. My parents-in-law seemed skeptical, but they asked no further questions about Ben.

While Pela and I had been away, my father had taken in a guest, an old business associate, Frank Piasecki, of Poznan. Mr. Piasecki had been one of the Polish Gentiles whom the Germans had expelled from their home towns in order to make room for citizens of the German *Reich*. In addition to inviting Mr. Piasecki to live with him until he could find a place of his own in Warsaw, my father had helped him set up a small store in one of the city's better neighborhoods, where he sold luggage, handbags and other leather goods. In those early days of the war, there still were Poles—Jews as well as Gentiles—who had the cash and the heart for such luxury items.

Shortly after our return, Mr. Piasecki left our apartment and rented an apartment of his own in the city.

Now that Pela and I had made up our minds to remain in Warsaw, I had to find work in order to make a living. The leather goods factory where I had been employed before the war had been bombed out. My father and my father-in-law had been unemployed since the beginning of the war because their places of work, too, had been destroyed by German bombs. Since then, my father and Pela's parents had managed to exist by selling their furniture, silver, china and other household goods piece by piece to get money for food and rent, but it was clear to me that they would not be able to go on in this fashion for long.

I got the idea to open a small toy and novelty store near our apartment building. Notwithstanding the war and its shortages, fathers and mothers still bought lead soldiers, mechanical toys and stuffed animals for their children. I found several toy manufacturers and wholesalers who had been bombed out of business and who were happy to sell me whatever remained of their stock. And so I went into business on my own, and soon was earning enough money to support Pela, our three parents and myself.

However, I saw that the situation of the Jews in Warsaw was deteriorating. The Gestapo began to arrest the elite of the Jewish community—doctors, lawyers and prominent businessmen. Also, they were picking up Jews from the streets at random for forced labor. This was in addition to the quota of Jewish men and women whom the *Judenrat* had to round up and make available to the Germans for work each day. Some of those who were seized in the streets were never seen again. Others reappeared in Warsaw with their arms or legs in casts, as a warning to those who would refuse to obey the Gestapo's orders.

There were reports of Jewish apartments and stores being looted by the Germans. A huge German army truck would pull up in front of a store and the owners themselves would be ordered to help the German soldiers load their merchandise onto the truck.

In addition to toys and novelties, I carried in my little store about 1,600 pairs of women's stockings which my father had salvaged from his place of work. (He had sold stockings along with his regular line of leather goods.) At this point the stockings represented a small fortune, which I did not want the Germans to get if they decided to loot my store. I therefore gave the whole lot to Mr. Piasecki to sell for us in the store which my father had helped him set up.

Before long Warsaw's Jewish community was faced with a serious housing shortage. Many Jews had been expelled from the rural areas and were streaming into Warsaw. The *Judenrat* appealed to the city's Jews to share their apartments with the newcomers. The *Ordnungsdienst*, the "Ghetto police" which had been organized by the *Judenrat* to enforce its directives, was in a position to compel Jewish families throughout the city to take in refugees because the *Judenrat* could use such coercive measures as withholding the bread rations of those who refused to cooperate.

Our wedding picture, May 31, 1936.

Pela and I, 1981

Now that Mr. Piasecki had left our three-room apartment, we had one room empty. We rented this room to two women, a mother and her daughter.

One morning late in February, 1940, as I left my apartment building to go to my store, I was caught in the street in a "Jew hunt." The German police assigned me to a group of Jews who were ordered to clear away the snow that covered the military parade grounds. At six o'clock that evening we were ordered to stop work on the parade grounds and taken to another neighborhood to clean the streets. After a while another young man and I agreed that we had done enough work for one day. We stepped out of formation without being noticed and made a dash for the courtyard of an apartment building nearby, where we hid until the long column of other Jews, flanked on either side by German policemen, had passed. Then we bade each other good night and I went home.

The idea that I should have been forced to do slave labor left me humiliated and depressed. I still had in my desk drawer the gun I had picked up on the highway to Brzesc. I vowed to myself that this was the last time I would be treated like a dog. Next time the Germans would not catch me alive. A few days later, I looked for my gun but it was no longer in my desk drawer. Eventually, I found out that Pela, who had noticed my bleak mood, had hidden the gun in the basement of our apartment building.

Early in the spring the Germans looted my store. The Gestapo arrived in a truck and forced me, at gunpoint, to load my merchandise onto the truck. Then they searched every corner and shelf of the store to make sure nothing had been left behind. That was the end of my first venture into business.

From that time on, our two households no longer had a regular source of income. Pela's parents, my father, Pela and I had to make do with the meager food rations which the *Judenrat* doled out to each Jewish family in Warsaw.

Early in May, 1940, Pela found out that she was pregnant. We received the news with mixed feelings. We considered it cruel to bring a child into the world in which we were now living. At the same time we could not help feeling pleased that Pela was able to have children. Before the war, when we had been newly married and desperately wanted a child, a doctor had told Pela that she would never be able to have a baby. That was the reason why Pela and I, unlike many of our friends, had not bothered to use birth control devices after the Germans had come. Now it turned out that the doctor had been mistaken, and we were happy and sad at the same time.

Several of our friends urged Pela to have an abortion. But neither my father nor Pela's parents would hear of it. Where there was new life, there was hope, they said, and Pela and I found ourselves agreeing with our parents. For a Jewish couple in Warsaw to have a baby in those days made life more complicated than it already was. The baby had to be fed, the mother needed good and ample nourishment, especially if she wanted to nurse the baby, and of course the baby was an added responsibility if the parents had to elude the Gestapo or were arrested. But at the same time, a baby was cherished as a token of trust in the future, symbolizing his parents' faith that mankind was not yet altogether lost and that there was hope for brighter days to come.

As spring turned into summer, rumors were rife that the Germans would move all the Jews of Warsaw into a ghetto. On July 1, 1940, the *Warschauer Zeitung*, mouthpiece of the German occupation authorities, published an order from Governor General Hans Frank that the city would be divided into three sections. The most desirable residential neighborhoods would be reserved for citizens of the German *Reich*—mostly military and civilian officials. The downtown section and most of the workers' suburbs would be assigned to Poles. The oldest, most rundown part of the city, the so-called "blighted area," would be the ghetto into which all the Jews in the city would be forced to move. The *Judenrat* bribed the Germans to postpone the establishment of the ghetto, but the reprieve was only temporary.

All that summer we could see Jews in the streets of Warsaw unloading bricks from trucks under the guns of the Gestapo. They would be ordered to build a wall on one street, only to be told to take it down again, brick by brick, and to rebuild it on some other street. We could not understand the purpose of this exercise. Some suggested that it was for civilian defense. How incredibly naive we were! But I was sure of one thing; nothing good was in store for us.

And so we went on living, or, more accurately, starving. We continued selling our household goods. There were always Jews who bought furniture for barter and then sold it to the Germans who were moving into Warsaw. We needed every penny we could get. Because of her pregnancy, Pela had to have good food and at least a little milk. One day her father went to his dentist and had several gold teeth extracted so he could sell them. With the money he was able to buy food on the black market, mostly for Pela.

On October 16, 1940, the Warsaw ghetto was established. All the Poles who were still living in the area set aside for the ghetto had to move out to make room for the Jews. The wall-building exercises which had gone on throughout the summer months had been practice operations to determine where the boundaries of the ghetto should be located.

The streets of the newly-established ghetto were scenes of terrible confusion. It was a nightmare. Over two hundred thousand Jews from all over Warsaw had to be moved into an area which already held at least a quarter of a million Jewish inhabitants, and 80,000 Poles who had to move out. Men, women, children, carrying on their backs whatever possessions they could take with them, jammed the streets of the ghetto. Some were pushing or pulling pushcarts piled high with their belongings. Meanwhile German soldiers stood on the sidewalks, taking pictures and movies and obviously enjoying the sight. Sometimes the Germans would turn over a pushcart, spilling its contents into the street and laughing uproariously as the unfortunate owner tried to raise his pushcart and reload it as quickly as he could.

We were lucky. Our apartment building was in the ghetto area so that we did not have to move.

I found out from a friend of mine, who had become active in the newly-organized Polish underground, that as of November 15, 1940 the Warsaw ghetto would be sealed. After that date Poles would not be permitted to enter the ghetto except by official authorization and Jews would not be allowed to go from the ghetto into the "Aryan sector" of the city. I therefore went immediately to the store of Frank Piasecki, which was in the "Aryan sector," and asked him to return to me whatever he still had left of the ladies' hose I had given him to sell. Piasecki gave me a thin smile and explained that he no longer had them. His store had been burglarized and the stockings had been among the merchandise that had been taken. When I told him that I had counted on the proceeds from the hose to pay the expenses connected with the birth of our baby, he merely shrugged his shoulders and said, with a sigh, that it would be much better if the child would never be born. I was convinced that Piasecki had lied about the stockings but I had no way of proving it. This was how Piasecki had repaid my father's kindness.

The reports about the plans for the sealing of the Warsaw ghetto were correct. In the morning of November 15, Jews who attempted to leave the ghetto to go to their places of work in the "Aryan sector" found the gates of the ghetto closed and heavily guarded by German police. The brick walls that had been built to mark the ghetto's boundaries had been topped with barbed wire and sharp slivers of glass. The ghetto had fourteen gates in all, which were guarded around the clock by German and Polish police. The German and Polish guards were assisted by the Jewish *Ordnungsdienst* of the *Judenrat*, who stood by to help preserve order and to act as interpreters for Jews who did not speak German.

When the word spread that the ghetto had been sealed, the Jews became panicky. Men huddled together in groups trying to figure out why the Germans would want to lock the Jews inside the ghetto. What did they want to do to the Jews? The women wept. Pela was distraught; she said she would never be able to forgive herself for having become pregnant. What sort of future could she possibly offer our unborn child?

A number of Jews were assigned by the Germans to work in the "Aryan sector" but they had to leave the ghetto each morning and return each evening, in groups, under police escort. Despite the fact that they were so closely supervised, these people developed an uncanny skill for smuggling food and other hard-to-obtain articles from the "Aryan sector" into the ghetto. Initially, there were no food shortages in the ghetto—provided one could afford to pay black market prices. Food brought in from the "Aryan sector" was less costly, although the

German and Polish police, of course, had to be bribed to turn a blind eye to the transactions. So-called "petty smugglers" spirited small packages of food into the ghetto. Poles would toss bags of potatoes, vegetables or groceries from the "Aryan sector" over the ghetto wall and the Jewish smugglers would be waiting near the wall inside the ghetto to catch the merchandise. Larger transactions were usually conducted at the Old Court House, which was at the edge of the ghetto and had two entrances—one on Leszno Street, which was in the ghetto, and the main entrance, which was on Ogrodowa Street, in the "Aryan sector." Although both entrances were closely guarded, it was possible to enter the building from either side under various pretexts.

On January 14, 1941, Pela gave birth to our daughter. Because we could not afford an obstetrician—even if we had known of one in the ghetto—the baby was delivered by a midwife. Pela lay on our dining room table. Since anaesthetics were beyond our means, Pela remained fully conscious throughout the delivery. As I watched Pela's features twist in pain, I was sure she would never survive. However, the baby was safely born. Pela and I swaddled her in a pillowcase around which we tied my father's belt. We named our daughter Jasia (Yanka) after Pela's grandfather, whose name had been Yankel.

The next day the midwife returned to suture Pela's episiotomy, again without an anaesthetic. Pela almost fainted but there were no complications and the baby, too, was doing well.

However, Pela's troubles were not yet over. She developed severe bursitis in her shoulder and an inflammation of the joints. For seven weeks she was in agony, without any medicine to give her relief. The pills she needed were unobtainable in the ghetto. My father and Pela's parents sold whatever they still possessed, mostly clothes, to street peddlers so that we could buy milk for the baby on the black market. We found a nurse-housekeeper to do the housework and to care for Pela and the baby. It was a woman who had moved into our apartment building with her six-year-old son. Her husband had died and she had no means of livelihood. We paid her with food for her little boy.

Meanwhile, the Germans continued to "resettle" Jews from the countryside in the Warsaw ghetto. Most of the apartments in the ghetto were already filled to capacity. The *Judenrat* converted schools, communal buildings and even synagogues into emergency shelters where the newcomers slept on the floor.

By this time bread rations in the ghetto had been reduced to half a pound per family every two or three days. The bread tasted like clay and was barely sufficient to afford an opportunity for slow death by starvation. The Jews in the various ghetto apartment buildings organized relief committees to help those less fortunate than themselves, if such distinctions could still be made. If there were indeed any "fortunates" in the Warsaw ghetto, our little family and Pela's parents could be counted among them. Both we and Pela's parents were still in the apartments where we had lived before the war, and we still had some possessions to sell or barter for food, unlike tens of thousands of others who had been expelled from their homes and had been forced to abandon all their property when they moved into the ghetto.

The ghetto was hit by a typhoid epidemic. Each time a new case was reported, the *Judenrat*'s health department put the patient's entire apartment building under quarantine for at least three days. Afterwards, every apartment in the building was subjected to a complicated and evil-smelling disinfection procedure.

67

Pela had not yet completely recovered from the birth of our baby and the illness that had followed. She was still barely able to walk. Nevertheless, she organized groups of tenants to go from apartment to apartment, collecting food and used clothing for the newcomers. She recruited other tenants as baby sitters to care for young children on a day-to-day basis.

Pela, whom I had always considered so delicate, proved hardier than I. It was not her health but mine that gave way at last. I developed a sore throat and a low-grade fever that hung on stubbornly. One day, when my temperature rose by one full degree, Pela went out to call the one ear, nose and throat specialist we knew in the ghetto. He came to our apartment and examined me. He said that my tonsils were badly infected and that they should be removed. However, he had neither the proper anaesthetics nor even all his surgical instruments. I decided to have him operate on me anyway because I could not take the chance of becoming seriously ill.

Like Pela's delivery, my operation took place in our dining room. I was seated on a chair, with my father pinning my arms to the back of the chair. Pela did not trust herself to watch. She left the apartment and waited in the street, in front of the building, until the doctor came out and told her that the operation was over. I opened my mouth as wide as I could and motioned to the doctor to go ahead. I cannot possibly describe the pain. Now, forty years later, when I have an ample supply of pills available to me for various minor twinges, I cannot understand how I survived the torture of that operation in Warsaw without an anaesthetic. I remember that the doctor was bathed in perspiration by the time he was done. But I was still a young man then and recovered within a few weeks.

Meanwhile, the smuggling traffic in food, and even in cows and horses, continued in the ghetto. Most of the larger contraband was now smuggled into the ghetto through the Jewish cemetery which bordered Okopowa Street on the west. The boundary of the ghetto ran along the east side of Okopowa Street so that, in fact, the Jewish cemetery was outside the ghetto area. Jews who wanted to bury their dead or to visit a grave in the cemetery had to obtain a special pass and could enter the cemetery only by way of the ghetto gate where Gesia Street, which ran east and west, met Okopowa.

Smuggling operations through the Jewish cemetery were conducted as follows: First, a contact was made between the Pole who had merchandise to sell and the Jew who wanted to buy it. Then a date and hour were set for the transaction. The parties would choose a time when the guard on duty at the ghetto gate on Gesia and Okopowa was someone whom they knew and who could be bribed to step aside or look away during the few minutes in which the transaction was made. Cows and horses, as a rule, were transported to the Jewish cemetery by way of the city's Catholic cemetery, which was directly adjacent to the Jewish burial ground. The two cemeteries were separated from one another by a partition which could easily be removed.

Though most of the smugglers in the ghetto were making a healthy profit from their operations, it must be remembered that many of the ghetto inhabitants who survived the war owe their lives to the supplies brought into the ghetto by smugglers.

Aside from the professionals, who dealt in large quantities of contraband and worked with substantial amounts of money, there were the "petty smugglers," who engaged in smaller deals. Some of the "petty smugglers" were boys and girls less than ten years old. These children would slip from the ghetto into the "Aryan sector" at certain unguarded places in the ghetto wall where enough bricks had been removed to make a hole through which one child could crawl in and out. Their "working clothes" included very roomy lined coats, and they might carry into the ghetto as much as 20 or 30 pounds of potatoes at one time, concealed under their coats or inside the linings. Darting back into the ghetto, they would hand the goods to the "customers" who had been waiting for them. Money changed hands and then the children returned to the "Aryan sector" for the next order. They could make several such trips in one day. Many of these boys and girls were, in fact, the sole support of their families, because potatoes brought good money. Every night these poor children, who had enjoyed so few good things during their short lives, returned to their parents' rooms in the ghetto tenements and proudly presented to their mothers the few pounds of potatoes which they had set aside for their own families and for which the grownups had been waiting anxiously all day long. Often, such children were caught by the Germans or were beaten up and robbed by Polish hoodlums as they slipped through their hole in the ghetto wall. Many of them were killed on the spot.

The Jews in the Warsaw ghetto were able to maintain a social life of sorts, mostly at night. During curfew hours, when Jews were not permitted in the streets, neighbors who lived in the same building would gather at each other's apartments. They would read German newspapers which had been smuggled into the ghetto from the "Aryan side" even though they knew that these papers contained only Nazi propaganda and reports of German victories on the African front. At one of these evening get-togethers in my own apartment building I proposed that all the tenants, as a group, should raise funds for the purchase of weapons and organize a Jewish self-defense group to go into action when the need, or the

70

opportunity, arose. But my suggestion was overruled; most of my neighbors felt that the only way to survive was to lie low and not offer active resistance to the Germans.

In June, 1941, the Germans launched a mass "collection" of furniture from the Jews in the ghetto. Their trucks, filled with Gestapo men, would pull up in front of an apartment building. While some of the men remained outside, guns at the ready, to surround the building, others went inside to search each apartment for good furniture. Then they would order the Jews to help load the furniture onto the trucks. Many families disguised their expensive mahogany or inlaid furniture with coats of cheap black or green paint to make it look inconspicuous and unattractive so that the Germans would not bother to take it.

When the Germans pulled up in front of our apartment building, Pela was prepared. She pasted on our apartment door a crudely-lettered quarantine sign reading "Fleckfieber"—the German term for typhoid fever. Typhoid fever was one of the very few things that could terrify even a hardened Gestapo man. The Germans did not try to enter our apartment that day.

Also in June, the Germans detached a large area from the ghetto, reassigning several wide avenues to the "Aryan sector." Among the streets thus arbitrarily excluded from the ghetto was the one in which Pela's parents lived. They were given one hour in which to vacate their apartment. They moved in with a family on Gesia Street, on the edge of the ghetto, near the Jewish cemetery.

The Germans were cracking down on the ghetto's smugglers. They assigned the most brutal of their SS men for guard duty at the ghetto gates. I particularly remember one SS man who was on guard at the gate which led to the Jewish cemetery. We referred to him as

"Frankenstein." As soon as he saw a Jew near the ghetto gate he would fire at him without warning. He had countless Jewish lives on his conscience.

By the summer of 1941 hunger was rampant in the Warsaw ghetto. To fill our growling stomachs we drank lots of water. Those who could afford it splurged on so-called *ersatz* tea, which was made by caramelizing a spoonful of precious sugar in a frying pan and then mixing the blackened sugar with a cupful of hot water. It tasted horrible, but sometimes Pela and I drank as many as 20 glasses of this brew in one single day.

Wherever one turned in the ghetto streets, one could see bodies lying on the spot where they had collapsed. They were bloated with malnutrition and their eyes were swollen shut. Some were half-naked because their clothes had been stripped from them by the living. They gave off a terrible, fetid smell. Several times each day workers from the Jewish cemetery made their rounds of the ghetto streets with pushcarts. They piled the dead, one atop the other, onto the pushcarts and wheeled them to the cemetery, where mass graves had been prepared for them. An average-size mass grave could accommodate several hundred bodies.

Our daughter, Jasia, was the one joy of our lives. She was now six months old, a beautiful baby with big, blue eyes and golden hair. Every time we looked at her our hearts ached to think that we did not know what the future held for her and that we were powerless to do anything to change that fact. Nevertheless it was Jasia who gave Pela and me the strength and incentive to survive.

Unfortunately Pela was too undernourished to nurse her adequately. I was determined that, for both Jasia's sake and her own, Pela must have good food. I began to make trips from the ghetto via the Jewish cemetery into the "Aryan sector" for milk and groceries. One of the workers in the Jewish cemetery gave me a pass stating that I was an employee of the cemetery. This pass made it possible for me to enter the cemetery at any time I chose without having to apply for a new pass on each occasion. Once in the cemetery, I would slip off my armband with the Star of David, climb a ladder and jump over the partition that separated the Jewish cemetery from the Catholic burial ground. From there I would emerge on Mlynarska Street in the "Aryan sector" and, because of my "Aryan" looks, was able to travel through the entire city, even on streetcars, without ever being stopped. I would buy enough butter and lard for my own family and Pela's parents, plus a little extra to sell to other families in the ghetto. I was badly in need of cash because I was now responsible for the support of eight persons—Pela, myself, Jasia, my father, Pela's parents, and the woman who had helped us during Pela's illness and who still lived in our building with her little son. Pela's parents did not live in our building, but they took most of their meals with us.

It was a real holiday for the seven of us—Jasia, of course, was still too young—when Pela could afford to buy half a kilogram of horsemeat and serve it for dinner. Such feasts were few and far between.

Pela and I felt it was our duty to help feed our other relatives as well. There was Pela's maternal grandmother, a woman of 70, who before the war had lived with Pela's younger married aunt in a villa in the suburb of Praga. Now the old woman, her daughter and her son-in-law lived together in a tiny apartment in the ghetto. Then there was my own mother's oldest sister, who lived not far from us with her husband and two sons. All the four of them were slowly starving to death. My uncle's legs and body were so bloated with hunger edema that he was hardly able to walk. For months he came to our apartment every day. Each time Pela would give him some food for himself and his family, often going without supper herself so that there would be enough for him.

One evening toward the end of August Pela went to my aunt's apartment with a jar of soup and a few dark rolls which I had bought in the "Aryan sector." When Pela entered my aunt's apartment with these delicacies, she found my uncle and aunt both lying on a mattress on the floor. (Their beds had been taken by the Germans in one of their periodic furniture "collections.") Their two young sons, their faces swollen from starvation, eagerly rose to welcome Pela and the food she brought, but the parents lacked the strength to rise from their mattress. Pela knelt down by the mattress and spoonfed them with the soup. Then she gave my aunt four rolls—one each for herself, my uncle and their two sons—and left. The next day we learned what had happened to my aunt's roll. Before going to sleep, my aunt gave one roll to each member of her family, saving her own roll to eat the next day. My uncle and the two boys ate their roll at once. That night, it seems, my poor uncle was unable to fall asleep. Seeing his wife's uneaten roll on the table proved too much of a temptation for him. He dragged himself from his side of the mattress and, in the dark, tried to reach for the roll on the table. He managed to grab the roll, but then apparently knocked his knee against a chair and fell. When my aunt awoke the next morning she found his lifeless body on the floor, his hand clutching her roll. He was taken to the Jewish cemetery and buried in a mass grave.

On December 25, Christmas Day 1941, the Gestapo issued an order that all Jews in the Warsaw ghetto had to deliver their furs and fur coats to the German occupation authorities no later than a specified date. After the deadline, it was announced, the Gestapo would search all

Jewish homes and if they found any furs "withheld" from them, they would execute the owner and his whole family. It seemed a rather stupid order because ninety per cent of those Jews in the Warsaw ghetto who had owned furs had sold them long ago for bread and other necessities of life.

Very early in the morning of January 2, 1942, I left home on one of my forays into the "Aryan sector." While I was away, my father tried to kill himself. At 7 o'clock, after I had left, Pela got up to warm some cereal for Jasia. She wondered why my father was not in his room. She thought that perhaps he had gone out, but it was not like him to leave home at such an early hour. When she wanted to go into the kitchen, she was surprised to find that the kitchen door was locked. She smelled gas. She pounded at the kitchen door with both her fists. When no answering sound came from the kitchen she rushed to our neighbors across the hall for help. They broke down our kitchen door. In the kitchen, my father lay on the floor, unconscious, with foam on his lips. He was still breathing, but his breath was shallow. While our neighbors attempted to revive him, the older of the two women who shared our apartment with us ran out of the house and hailed a rickshaw—the ghetto's one remaining mode of public transportation—to fetch an ambulance; there were hardly any private telephones left in ghetto apartments. It so happened that our tenant noticed me in the street. She signaled to me frantically to get into the rickshaw with her. She told me about my father and, together, we got an ambulance which took my father to the ghetto hospital.

Conditions in that hospital were chaotic. Most of the drugs and all but the most primitive equipment had been taken away by the Germans. The doctors fought for ten days to save my father. It seemed as if he had lost the will to live; he alternated between unconsciousness and drowsy lethargy. On the eleventh day he spoke for the first time. "Why didn't you let me die?" he asked.

On January 14, Jasia became one year old, but no one was in the mood to celebrate her birthday. Not only was my own father in the hospital, but Pela's father had sunk into a deep depression. He told me he had never really believed the story in Martin Gingold's letter that Ben was alive and probably on his way to Palestine. With tears in his eyes he begged me to tell him the truth about his son. He promised that if the news was bad, he would keep it between us; he would never tell his wife. But I stuck to my story. I did not want to deprive my parents-in-law of the one hope that might keep them alive: the dream of a reunion with their son after the war. My father-in-law never asked me about Ben again. As for my mother-in-law, I think she willed to believe my story. Perhaps she felt that if she would ever question me and I would put an end to her hopes she would not be able to survive. And so she said nothing to me about Ben and devoted all her love and concern to her grandchild, our little Jasia.

We brought my father home from the hospital. He had suffered no permanent physical damage, but he was no longer what he had been before the war and my mother's death. He appeared indifferent to the world about him and Pela and I watched him very closely because he clearly felt that he had been made to survive against his will.

7

On February 12, 1942, after dark, following a day's search for food in the "Aryan sector," I was ready to return to the ghetto through the Jewish cemetery. Suddenly a voice directly behind me shouted, *"Halt! Hände hoch!*

(Stop! Put up your hands!)" and I heard the click of a machine gun readied for action.

I put up my hands, turned around and was momentarily blinded by the beam of a flashlight. When the hand that held the flashlight moved slightly to one side, I saw an SS man staring straight at me. He ordered me to face the cemetery wall and stretch my arms until the tips of my extended fingers touched the wall. Then he searched me for weapons. For a split second I was tempted to wheel around and fling myself at him. If I took the SS man by surprise, I thought, I would stand a chance of escaping. If my attempt failed, at least I would be shot at once and I would be spared the humiliation of imprisonment and torture. But then I remembered Pela and our baby, and I told myself that I had no right to throw my life away before it was taken from me. As long as I remained alive, there was hope for the three of us. And so I stood quietly, arms extended in front of me to touch the cemetery wall.

I remained standing in this position for almost an hour, with the SS man holding his gun behind me. Then I heard the motor of an approaching car. Four SS men appeared out of the shadows. They seized me, spun me around and pushed me into a Gestapo car. I was taken to a Gestapo station at the corner of Wronia and Chlodna Streets. There, the SS men prodded me up a flight of steps with the barrels of their guns. On the second floor, they escorted me, with their gun barrels cold against my back, into a large office. I saw two desks, behind each of which sat a Gestapo officer. Despite their well-tailored dress uniforms, these two Nazis looked like perfect models for a "Wanted" poster in a United States post office.

I was ordered to stand at attention in the center of the office. I was no longer afraid of what would happen to me. I was worried only about Pela and the baby. What would become of them if I would not come home? But now there was nothing I could do to save myself. I could feel nothing but utter despair. Only a few weeks earlier, my father had attempted suicide. If I failed to return home, he would almost certainly make another try, and this time Pela would probably join him. I reproached myself for having brought a child into this world of horrors.

"*Bist du Jude?* (Are you a Jew?)" one of the two Gestapo officers barked from behind his desk. I looked at him. He was about 30 years old and wore steel-rimmed glasses. "*Ja, ich bin Jude* (Yes, I am a Jew)," I replied.

The officer leaped from his chair, walked around his desk toward me and kicked me in the groin. I saw stars before my eyes. I staggered but managed to keep myself from falling. I knew that if I fell, the Gestapo men would finish me off immediately. The first spasm of excruciating physical pain was followed by a fit of helpless rage. If only I could shout out what I thought of the Gestapo and of all the Nazis! If only I could throw something—anything—into the faces of those two Nazis, I thought, I would feel relieved. Even if they would kill me. But once again I remembered Pela and Jasia, and I said and did nothing.

The Gestapo man who had kicked me returned to his seat behind his desk. He ordered me to empty the pockets of my pants and jacket and put their contents on his desk. I did as I was told. Now the Gestapo man was calm, almost civilized. Apparently he felt better for having been able to kick me.

He pawed through my wallet and pulled out a snapshot of Jasia, taken by a neighbor in the ghetto who was fortunate enough not only to have a camera from before the war but also to possess films that were still in usable condition. The Gestapo man looked at the picture.

"*Wer ist dieses dreckige Kind?* (Who is this filthy child?)," he wanted to know.

"*Das ist kein dreckiges Kind. Das ist meine kleine Tochter* (That's not a filthy child. This is my little daughter)," I replied.

The Gestapo man rose from his seat and gave me a resounding slap in the face. I repeated that as far as I was concerned, Jasia was the most beautiful, precious child on earth and no one had the right to call her filthy.

The Gestapo man guffawed. He took an automatic revolver from his desk drawer and began to play with it. His colleague, seated at the other desk, now took over. He interrogated me. What was my name? My address? And what had I been doing in the "Aryan sector"? Didn't I know that the "Aryans" didn't want filthy Jews from the ghetto mixing with them? I played the guileless fool. I had a friend in the "Aryan sector," I said, a Polish Catholic who had gone to school with me. I had wanted to visit him and ask him to help me get some food for my baby. However, I added, I had not been able to find him, for when I came to the street where he lived, I saw only rubble in the place where his apartment building had once been. I invented this sad detail on the spur of the moment because I hoped it would sound credible to my interrogator and would dissuade the Gestapo from attempting to check whether I really had such a friend in the "Aryan sector."

My interrogator told me that I was too impudent for my own good and that he would teach me how to answer properly when spoken to. I thought he would hit me, but he merely pushed a buzzer on his desk. An SS man entered the room, grabbed my arm and led me down a flight of stone steps into a bare prison cell. Then he turned on his heel, walked out of the cell and locked the door behind him.

The cell was bare except for a cot. I sat down on the cot, wondering what would happen next. About half an hour later the door of the cell was unlocked and another SS man entered. He grabbed my arm, jerked me to my feet and led me out of the cell.

My next stop was an odd-looking room. My SS escort left me there with the parting announcement that I would soon be taken care of. I looked around the room. It was a torture chamber that reminded me of horror stories I had read in school about prisons during the Middle Ages. It was a small, windowless room, about eight feet square, lit by a bare bulb screwed into a wall outlet near the ceiling. The walls were spattered with what looked like dried blood. There were several iron stools, and some heavy chains beside them on the floor. In one corner stood a long wooden bench with pieces of broken glass glued to its seat. The slivers of glass, too, bore traces of blood. I could not help thinking that the Germans must consider us Jews a special breed if they took the trouble to devise such elaborate means for getting rid of us.

"*Ausziehen!* (Undress!)" a voice barked outside. Once again, the rebel inside me demanded his due. I did not take off my clothes. Let the Germans come in and do the job themselves, I thought. The worst thing they could do to me for disobeying orders would be to shoot me right then and there. Better a sudden end than unending torture, I told myself. So I shouted to the German outside that he could do to me whatever he wanted but that I would not take off my clothes in this room.

Then the unexpected happened. The SS man opened the door of the torture chamber, walked in and said to me, "I merely wanted to show you this place. Plenty of Jews have already been bumped off in this room. But I think you've had enough for today. We can wait till tomorrow to bring you back here and get you to talk." With these words he led me out of the torture chamber

80

and back into the cell where I had been before. Then he left me, locking the door behind him. I was too bewildered to think, let alone sleep.

Sometime during the night my cell door was unlocked and a new SS man walked in. "*Komm mit!* (Come with me!)," he said curtly. I went with him. I thought I was going to be taken back to the torture chamber. But to my amazement the SS man led me up the flight of stone steps I had descended only a few hours earlier, and I found myself passing through the gate of the Gestapo building, out into the street. I could not believe my eyes, but the mere fact that I was no longer inside the Gestapo building gave me new hope. Also, in striking contrast to his colleagues, this SS man seemed almost human. He explained to me that he had received orders to hand me over to the Polish police and that he was therefore taking me to the Central Headquarters of the Warsaw police force. As we walked, he kept talking to me. He said he felt sorry for me because he knew very well that I was not a criminal. He did not say anything about my being a Jew. As far as he was concerned, he said he would not mind if I escaped, but he could not turn me loose because then the Gestapo would shoot him and he wanted so badly to go back to his wife and children in Germany.

I asked him why the Gestapo should want to hand a Jew over to the Polish police. He answered that the Gestapo in Warsaw considered it a waste of time to deal with Jews who had been arrested in "routine operations." Therefore, except in cases where a Jew had been charged officially with a major crime, such as murder, Jews arrested by the Gestapo were generally transferred to the custody of the Polish police. Of course, the Polish police was responsible to the Gestapo authorities, but I was relieved because I could not imagine that the Polish police would subject me to the indignities I could have expected in a Gestapo prison.

At Central Police Headquarters several policemen stopped to greet me and to ask me why I had been arrested. They even addressed me as *pan* ("Mister") and informed me that I was lucky to be out of the Gestapo's hands and in the custody of the Polish police. "You'll be safe with us," one of them said. "At least for the time being."

Several minutes later, a Polish policeman escorted me out of Central Police Headquarters and walked with me to the Third District Police Station, which was located inside the ghetto area. It was, in fact, on Novolipki Street, close to my apartment building. The policeman was unarmed, except for a wooden night stick. It occurred to me that it should not be too difficult to run away from him, but I realized that I was still on the Gestapo books and that if the Gestapo would spread a dragnet to recapture me, it would be the end not only for me but also for Pela, our baby and our parents.

However, I asked my policeman for a favor. Since we were practically going to pass the apartment building in which I lived, would he permit me to go up to my apartment to tell my wife what had happened to me and where I was going? I promised that he would be well compensated for his cooperation. He agreed to let me stop at my apartment, provided I would make no trouble about going to the police station with him afterwards.

Followed by my escort, I climbed up the steps to my apartment. I had to knock for quite a while before the door opened. Both Pela and my father were at the door. Their eyes were red and swollen; they had given me up for dead. They had expected me to come home, as usual, at about 6 or 7 in the evening, and now it was 3 o'clock the next morning. Pela tried to smile, but without much success, for when she saw the Polish policeman standing close beside me she knew at once what I would have to tell her.

The policeman said I would have ten minutes to say my farewells to my family. He was not a bad sort. He even attempted to reassure Pela that I would be out of prison soon. In fact, he gave her the name of a police officer, Lieutenant Slivinsky, a Pole of German origin, who, he said, was a decent fellow and had considerable influence with the Gestapo authorities. The policeman suggested that Pela turn to him for help.

Meanwhile, I bent over the crib where our baby Jasia was sound asleep. As I kissed her I vowed to myself that I would make every effort to survive until the war was over, so I could see to it that she and other children like her would have a future of peace and security. Then, pretending a lightheartedness I did not feel, I kissed Pela good-by and said to her, "See you soon."

At the Third District Police Station I was locked into a cell, but after the Gestapo torture chamber it did not seem too bad. The sergeant on duty offered me some food, but I did not feel like eating. I was told that I would be kept at this police station until my Gestapo file arrived, which might take several days. After that, I would be transferred to the military prison on Gesia Street.

At five o'clock in the morning, less than two hours after I had left her, the door of my prison cell was unlocked and Pela entered, carrying a large paper bag. It contained a canister of black coffee, black bread and some cigarettes—the latter a gift from the House Committee, the group of neighbors elected in each ghetto apartment building to see to the needs of all the tenants. Pela told me that none of our neighbors had slept that night, and that some of them had spent the evening with her and my father to wait with them until they could learn what had happened to me.

That very day Pela contacted Lieutenant Slivinsky and offered him our bedroom furniture as a gift if he would secure my release. He replied that while such a gift was really not sufficient to compensate him for such a risky effort, he would try to do what he could for me.

The next day, February 14, Slivinsky visited me. He asked me several questions and coached me in what I should say when I would be interrogated.

Later that day I was taken out of my cell and escorted, again on foot, back to the Central Police Headquarters building, where the interrogation took place. Like Lieutenant Slivinsky, the officer who questioned me was a *Volksdeutscher*. I was grilled as thoroughly as if I had been a notorious gangster captured after a long and dangerous manhunt.

Afterwards, I was transferred to the military prison on Gesia Street. This prison, too, was within the area assigned to the ghetto. As my escorts and I approached the prison, I saw Pela standing near the gate. She started to move toward me, but a German officer noticed it and rudely pushed her aside.

When the gate of the prison clanged shut behind me, I was overcome by a feeling of helplessness. I felt as if I had been suddenly paralyzed. I had never seen the inside of a prison before, and here I was, arrested and jailed like a common criminal, for trying to find a little food for my wife and my baby.

After a routine body search and another interrogation, I was led to my cell. It was a small cell. Also, it did not have an inch of space to spare, for it already held eighteen other prisoners. I was to be the nineteenth.

I quickly became acquainted with my cellmates, all Jews, of course. I found out that most of the Jews in the Gesia Street prison were better types—doctors, lawyers and businesspeople, plus a few young boys who had been caught smuggling potatoes into the ghetto.

Most of the time, my cellmates and I were too depressed to talk. Our daily prison fare was simple. For breakfast, at five o'clock in the morning, a piece of black bread, which tasted like clay and which we washed down with a mug of *ersatz* coffee. At noon came a small bowl of watery soup, and at five in the afternoon another cup of man-made coffee. The bread we got each morning was the only solid food we received, and we were expected to make it last until "afternoon coffee." But of course no one, at least not in my cell, could muster the will power to save any part of the bread for twelve hours. We ate it all in the morning and then spent most of the day lying on the cold stone floor of our cell. Our families were not permitted to visit us or to send us food.

I remained in this cell for about eight weeks. On April 14, without any previous warning, I was summoned to the interrogation room. A Polish policeman was waiting for me there. After making some brief notations on an official form, he told me that I was free to go home.

I could hardly believe my ears. I was so overjoyed, in fact, that I forgot the hunger pangs which had been plaguing me constantly for two months. When the prison gates closed behind me and I was in the street alone, without a police escort, I took a deep breath. What a pleasure it was to breathe fresh air again, even if it was only the air of the ghetto! Once again my philosophy of life had proven itself: as long as I was alive, there was hope for me and my family.

As I turned the corner of Gesia Street, there was Pela, running to meet me. Lieutenant Slivinsky had sent word to her that I had been released and she had given him our bedroom set as she had promised. Slivinsky, it turned out, had obtained my release from Gesia Street by a bureaucratic trick; he had exchanged my papers for those of a

Polish thief who was supposed to be in another prison, not in the "Jewish jail" on Gesia Street.

My freedom was to last for a little less than three months.

8

During the spring months of 1942, as the weather grew warmer, a new sight became increasingly frequent in the streets of the Warsaw ghetto: groups of SS men operating movie cameras. It was rumored that they had been sent by Dr. Joseph Goebbels' Ministry of Propaganda in Berlin to take movies of the happy, prosperous life which the Polish Jews were leading under German occupation. The moviemen first went to the Jewish cemetery, where they ordered the Jewish gravediggers to bring out an elaborate hearse which had been used at funerals of wealthy Jews before the war. Next, they produced a pair of handsome black horses, hitched them to the hearse and ordered two Jewish wagon drivers to put on their prewar frock coats and mount the driver's seat. Then, with the help of the Polish police and the *Ordnungsdienst* of the *Judenrat*, the SS movie team staged an elaborate funeral procession, complete with a cast of mourners, consisting of Jews hand-picked from the streets because they happened to be wearing halfway decent clothing. The only prop missing was the corpse. In all likelihood this production was subsequently presented at movie theaters all over Germany to show the grand style in which Warsaw's Jews could still afford to bury their dead.

Other German propaganda films produced in the Warsaw ghetto were intended to portray the immorality of the Jewish race. As the cast for these productions the Germans would select elderly Jewish men, preferably the

86

bearded, Orthodox type, and young girls between the ages of 14 and 18. At the point of their machine guns, the Germans would herd these men and girls together into a *mikvah*, the bathhouse used by religious Jews for their ritual ablutions. Men and women never bathe in the *mikvah* pools together. Married women perform their immersions at the end of each monthly period to purify themselves for their husbands; the men come at other times, particularly before the major holidays, to cleanse themselves for worship. But now the Germans ordered the old men and the young girls to undress and to bathe together naked in the pool in a variety of indecent positions. Those who refused to obey were shot at once.

I myself witnessed preparations for what I consider one of the most disgusting anti-Jewish propaganda films produced by the Germans. One day early in May, as I was walking on Karmelicka Street, I saw a mob scene. The Gestapo was rounding up Jewish men and women whose clothes were still better than rags and who had not yet acquired the emaciated look of the starving creatures we would see dead each day on the sidewalks of the ghetto. This hand-picked "cast" was escorted to Schultz's Restaurant on the corner of Karmelicka and Novolipki Streets, which before the war had been a fine Jewish restaurant popular for its tasty meals. The restaurant had been closed since the outbreak of the war, but now the Germans "reopened" it temporarily for their own purposes. Tables were set with dazzling white tablecloths, gleaming silverware and dainty china, and a turkey dinner was produced with all the trimmings, including bottles of choice wines and liqueurs. All the fancy food and tableware had, of course, been imported by the Germans in trucks from the "Aryan sector."

Some members of the "cast" were ordered to put on white jackets—also supplied by the Gestapo—and to play the role of waiters, while others were commanded to sit down as "guests" at the dinner tables and start eating. After these preliminaries had been set up, the Gestapo brought to the restaurant a second contingent of "actors": beggars and other Jews whose clothes hung in tatters and whose faces and bodies bore visible signs of starvation. These living skeletons were ordered to hover around the tables and beg the "guests" for some food. The "guests" had to push the beggars away from the tables and the "waiters" had to complete the act by throwing the beggars out of the restaurant. The purpose of this film, of course, was to show that there were still plenty of rich Jews left in the ghettoes, and that they had no feelings of compassion for the poor, not even for their own fellow Jews.

As soon as the filming was over, the Germans ordered the "cast" to load the restaurant equipment and the food back onto the Gestapo trucks. The Jews were not permitted to take so much as one piece of bread from the elaborate display.

On May 5, trouble came to our apartment building. A Gestapo car pulled up at the entrance. Two SS men entered the building and broke into the apartment of our neighbors, the Orensteins, whose windows and balcony faced ours. The Orensteins had an only child, an eight-year-old girl, Judith. Before the war, Mr. Orenstein, like so many others in our building, had been in the leather goods business. Later Mrs. Orenstein, in hysterics, told us what happened to her husband and child.

It seemed that a Jewish collaborator had reported to the Gestapo that her husband still had in his apartment some leather from his store. Leather at the time was at a premium, and the Germans were anxious to get their hands on every scrap available. When Mr. Orenstein protested that he had none of his stock left (which was the truth), the SS men began to beat him with their leather whips. Little Judith tried to throw herself at the Germans. "Stop hitting my father!" she cried. But the SS men only laughed and started beating the child, too. Then one of the SS men shot Mr. Orenstein and threw the child from the balcony.

Four days later, on May 9, the Germans came for me. At about 10 o'clock that morning Pela went out for a short walk with Jasia. About fifteen minutes after they had left, a Gestapo car pulled up in front of our apartment building. Moments later, there was a knock on our door. I opened and saw two young SS men, each carrying a machine gun. "*Komm mit!* (Come with us!)" they said. I told them that I wanted to go to the bathroom first. "Don't try any of your Jewish tricks on us," one of the SS men barked, "unless you want to see the blood of your family running all over this floor!" I did not go to the bathroom. My father wanted to kiss me good-by but the SS men pushed him away with the butts of their guns.

Meanwhile, Pela had returned with the baby and saw the Gestapo car in front of our building. She rushed up the stairs with Jasia in her arms just as the SS men slammed the apartment door behind me. Holding Jasia tightly to her, she began to scream in Polish at the SS men, calling them the vilest names in the Polish dictionary. I breathed a silent prayer that the Germans should take me away as quickly as possible so they would not hear Pela any more. I knew that if by some chance either of these two Germans understood Polish, it would be the end of Pela.

The SS men seized my arms and rushed me down the steps. Outside, they hustled me into their car and drove me to the Gestapo station at Wronia and Chlodna Streets. Just as three months earlier, so now, too, I was led into the interrogation room. This time there were three German officers—not just two—waiting for me. One of them rose from his seat behind his desk, marched up to me and hit me on the right cheek with a hard rubber truncheon. I became dizzy and felt a sharp pain in my head, but once again, like the last time, I took care to keep myself from falling.

The Germans kept me standing for about ten minutes. No one spoke. Then another one of the three officers got up from his seat. "How did you ever get out of jail, you Jewish swine?" he bellowed, and started beating me with his truncheon. I finally fainted. I do not remember how long I remained unconscious, but I was awakened by a shower of cold water from a bucket. I was ordered to get up and stand at attention. Then one of the officers asked me who I thought would win the war, the Germans, or the British and American swine. Before I had a chance to open my mouth in reply, I was knocked down again and given about 20 blows on my buttocks with a rubber truncheon.

This supposed "interrogation" continued for almost an hour. It was now past noon. I was escorted to the Gesia Street military prison, where I had been taken also in February, but this time I did not go under my own power. The Germans had to drag me through the streets because blood was pouring from my nose and mouth and I was no longer able to stand on my legs.

I was put into a cell with eight other inmates. I recognized two of them. One, an older man, was a doctor who had lived in our neighborhood. The other was a salesman who had frequently visited the leather goods factory where I had worked before the war. But we did not have much to say to each other. During my months of freedom I had heard rumors that the cells in this prison were now bugged and that any prisoners who talked about the treatment they had received would be shot at once.

My brother Henry (+) with his Maccabi group greeted by Mayor Meir Dizengoff after their arrival in Tel Aviv on motorcycles from Warsaw (1933).

Our daughter Joanne (Jasia), a few months after our arrival in Chicago

1948: My brother Henry in Israel, as a member of the Haganah, the underground Jewish defense force

None of my fellow inmates wore a prison uniform. I, too, was allowed to keep the clothes in which I had been arrested. This was to prove a lucky thing for me.

During my first night in the cell I could not sleep at all. Every muscle in my body was still so sore from the "interrogation" that I could not even lie down on the floor without feeling the pain.

At five o'clock the next morning we were served the breakfast I remembered from my first time in the Gesia Street prison—bread and *ersatz* coffee. Then the door of our cell creaked open and two SS men walked in. They looked around and after a while pointed their fingers at four of the men in the cell. *"Raus mit euch!* (Out!)"* they shouted. Among the four chosen were the doctor and the salesman.

Fifteen minutes later we heard gunfire from the prison yard. The four men who had left the cell never returned. In the afternoon, three new prisoners were brought into our cell.

I had never witnessed such a procedure during the eight weeks I had spent at this prison before. Later, I was to learn that this was a newly-devised ritual of torture that took place in every cell at breakfast time each morning. The prisoners to be shot were picked at random by the SS men, so that the life of each prisoner was at stake each morning and depended on the mood of the SS men who happened to call at his cell that day.

Meanwhile Pela, in desperation, went to Central Headquarters of the Polish police to tell Lieutenant Slivinsky that I had been arrested again. She hoped he might be able to get me out this time, too. At police headquarters she was told that the lieutenant was not in. But in the corridor she met a Polish policeman who happened to know her parents. After hearing her story, the policeman told Pela that he had a friend on duty at the Gesia Street prison and that he would ask him to find out whether I was there. "Come back tomorrow, *Pani* Starkopf," he said. "I should have news for you by then."

Pela hardly slept that night. Very early the next morning she set out on foot for police headquarters to meet the policeman. In the street, she saw that something was terribly wrong. Women were standing in front of apartment buildings, still dressed in their bathrobes, their hair disheveled. They were screaming hysterically. Passers-by stopped to ask what had happened. Pela soon knew the answer. That night, for the first time, the German "death car" had made the rounds of the ghetto streets. The "death car" was a shiny black limousine with a skull and crossbones painted on the door. It was the latest torture instrument devised by the Germans and it worked as follows:

The Gestapo had compiled a list of the names and addresses of Jews in the Warsaw ghetto who had been wealthy or socially prominent before the war. Between four and five o'clock each morning, the "death car" would pull up at addresses chosen at random from this Gestapo list. The heads of the wanted families would be pulled from their beds and, still in their night clothes, would be dragged out into the street. There, in front of their apartment buildings, they would be shot in the back of the head at such close range that they were mutilated beyond recognition.

That first night, Pela later learned, about 50 Jews had been killed. Among them was a man who had owned a large bakery before the war and had lived in our street.

As always, the Germans were efficient. The dead were not permitted to remain in the street for long. Each time the "death car" left on its rounds, the Gestapo would telephone the office of the Jewish cemetery, requesting that workers with pushcarts report no later than 5:30 A.M. at the apartment buildings on the "death list" for that day to pick up the bodies of those shot. By the time Pela came out into the street that first morning, all she saw was the mourning; the dead were no longer to be seen.

From that time on the ghetto population was in a constant state of panic. The Jews were afraid to sleep in their own beds at night. They slept in attics and basements. Nevertheless, the "death cars" continued to reap their harvest. Eventually, the Gestapo sent out "extermination details" also during the daytime. One of our friends, a Mr. Gory, was killed in broad daylight on Leszno Street. When his mother, who happened to be with him, threw herself in front of her son to protect him, the Germans blew her brains out also.

Before long the Germans expanded these operations into mass "actions," picking up Jews at random, herding them into trucks, driving them out of the ghetto into an empty space somewhere in the "Aryan sector" and shooting them there, dozens at a time. These victims, too, were shot at close range so that their bodies could not be identified.

Meanwhile, at the Gesia Street prison, the daily executions continued. Each morning, when the door of my cell creaked open, I was certain that my turn had come to die. I had resigned myself to the probability that I would never see my wife and child again.

Informed by the policeman that I was in the Gesia Street prison again, Pela worked feverishly to secure my release. But this time Lieutenant Slivinsky never seemed to be available. Finally, because she did not know where else to turn for help, Pela paid a visit to an individual whom everyone in the ghetto regarded as something less than human: a Jewish informer who was known in the ghetto as Yossele Kapote. Before the war, Yossele had been what was called in Yiddish a *treger*, a porter who hired out his pushcart and his muscles for moving furniture or other household goods from one building to another. This was considered one of the lowliest of menial occupations among the Jews of Warsaw. Yossele was not only a rude, uncouth character but was widely rumored to have accumulated a police record before the war. But now, in the ghetto, Yossele was a big shot, proudly sporting an official-looking cap adorned with four stars. No one seemed to know what these stars were supposed to signify, but everyone knew that Yossele Kapote had become very popular with the Gestapo. He was one of those despicable creatures who thought he would be able to save his own hide and to make good money by informing on his own people. Yossele lived on our street with a Jewish prostitute whom he had taken as his mistress. He made a good living as a Gestapo stool pigeon, but at the same time, rumor had it, he could be persuaded to use his privileged status to help get Jews out of trouble—provided it brought him enough cash.

And so one day Pela, accompanied by my father, called on Yossele Kapote at his apartment. Yossele was not in, but his girl friend was there, lunching on such delicacies as scrambled eggs, sardines, chocolate milk and cake. While decent, innocent people round about her were starving to death, this scum, this traitor to her own people, was living off the fat of the land.

Pela and my father were graciously permitted to sit at the table with Yossele's girl friend and to watch her eat. Finally, after she had enjoyed the last morsel of her chocolate cake, the woman asked Pela what she wanted. When Pela told her my story, she said, "Don't worry, *Pani* Starkopf. Your husband is in no danger. German prisons aren't as bad as they are made out to be." Then, after a pause, she continued, "However...if you happen to have some cash—say, about 10,000 zlotys—Yossele might be able to arrange something."

94

Pela looked at her without uttering a word, then turned to my father and said to him, "Come, Papa, let's get out of here. If there is any justice left in this world, I hope the ghosts of the people whom her fine friend sent to their death will haunt her until she dies." My father tried to calm Pela down. He was afraid that Yossele's girl friend could have Pela arrested also. But Pela did not stop screaming curses at Yossele and his mistress even in the street. When my father gently pleaded with her to be quiet, she cried out that she no longer cared whether or not she would be arrested. She was sure that I was lost, and she saw no point in attempting to survive without me.

One night, in the middle of June, 1942, after I had been in prison a month, the corridor outside my cell echoed with the tramp of heavy boots. The SS was staging a night raid. We could hear cell doors creaking open and the screams of prisoners as they were dragged out of their cells. For a moment, the SS men stopped in front of our cell. My cellmates and I exchanged looks of silent farewell, convinced that our time had come. But the door of our cell remained locked. After moments during which time seemed to stand still, the SS men turned on their heels and went on. We could not understand why we should have been spared. Later, we learned through the prison grapevine—which operated remarkably well despite rumors that each cell was bugged—that 100 men had been taken out of the Gesia Street prison that night for execution. Unlike those "selected" during the daily morning visitations, the victims of this special raid had not been shot in the prison yard but had been driven in trucks to the Jewish cemetery to be gunned down wholesale. As Pela told me later, the Gestapo then plastered the walls and fences of the ghetto with posters announcing that 100 young men had been executed at the Gesia

Street prison because they did not fit into the new order of the German Reich.

Meanwhile, life—or death—went on in the Warsaw ghetto. The Germáns completed their plans for the mass deportation of Jews from the Warsaw ghetto to Treblinka. The village of Treblinka was about 60 miles northeast of Warsaw, not far from Malkinia, the railroad junction where, on New Year's Day, 1940, Pela and I had boarded the train for Warsaw following the tragic end of our search for Ben. In December, 1941 the Germans had built in Treblinka a prison camp which they named Treblinka I. Now, in the spring of 1942, they had set up an additional camp about a mile away from the original Treblinka. They named this new camp Treblinka II. As distinct from Treblinka I, where the prisoners were used for slave labor and their death was regarded as a mere "by-product," Treblinka II was expressly designed for the mass destruction of its inmates. Treblinka II was the camp to which Jews were deported from the Warsaw ghetto. Only a handful managed to escape and subsequently lived to tell the horrors they saw at this death factory, where nearly a million Jews lost their lives.

But until the summer of 1942, only few Jews, if any, knew the truth about Treblinka. Many of the Jews in the Warsaw ghetto were tricked into "volunteering" for deportation, or death, or both.

Early in the summer of 1942 the Germans advised all Jews in the Warsaw ghetto who were citizens of neutral countries to register with the occupation authorities.

In the middle of July, 1942, the Germans posted bulletins throughout the Warsaw ghetto announcing that all Jews who had registered with the authorities as citizens of neutral countries were to report, with their families and their belongings, at a designated place from which they would be transferred to Pawiak, one of Warsaw's largest prisons. A small number of those Jews who really were citizens of neutral countries were eventually transferred out of Poland into Vichy France and from there managed to make their way to freedom.

That same month—in July, 1942—the foreigners were joined at Pawiak by a contingent of Warsaw Jews, intellectuals and also several members of the *Judenrat*, who had been arrested as hostages.

On July 22, 1942, the Germans began the first of a series of *Aktionen*, or mass deportations. No one knew it then, but this was the first step in the projected liquidation of the Warsaw ghetto. Aided by Ukrainian helpers and armed with machine guns, the Germans first descended on the ghetto's hospitals, old age homes, refugee shelters and orphanages, ordered the inmates out and herded them into trucks that stood waiting in long columns. The sick and the aged were driven directly to the Jewish cemetery, where mass graves had been dug to receive them. They were lined up in front of the mass graves and shot. The explanation for this procedure was that the sick and the old were of no value to anyone, including themselves, because they were not fit for work in labor camps.

Meanwhile, acting on the orders of the Gestapo, the *Judenrat* put up posters throughout the ghetto reassuring the Jews that they would come to no harm. The Gestapo was going to round up Jews, but merely for purposes of "resettlement"; they would be taken away from the overcrowded ghetto and moved to the eastern part of Nazi-occupied Poland, where they would be given work and shelter in camps set up especially for them. Side by side with these posters from the *Judenrat* were other posters, issued by the German occupation authorities. These posters called upon all Jews in Warsaw to report on their own accord for "resettlement." Everyone who would report voluntarily would receive three kilograms of bread and a kilogram of marmalade as a reward for promptness. This offer seemed most tempting to the starving Jews of the ghetto. Many young, healthy individuals were only too ready to believe what they read, and so they volunteered for their own deportation to the death camp of Treblinka.

The Germans worked quickly on those days in July. After the hospitals, the old age homes, the refugee shelters and the orphanages had been evacuated, it was the turn of Pawiak prison and the other prisons in the ghetto area. Among those prisons was the Gesia Street military prison where I was now "serving" my third month. The Germans came for us late in the afternoon. The building was surrounded by SS units armed to the teeth. SS men broke into the prison, emptied the cells and marched all the inmates, cell by cell, into the prison yard. Within a matter of hours, thousands of prisoners, including myself, had been assembled in the yard. The Germans had added a new refinement to their methods of torture. They had trained police dogs to attack Jews on command. The word "Jude! (Jew!)" was sufficient to goad the beasts into action. As I emerged from the prison into the yard I saw the bodies of prisoners who had been torn to pieces by the dogs.

For some reason, the much-touted SS efficiency failed to work at the Gesia Street prison that day. In their zeal to empty the prison as quickly as possible, the Germans had apparently forgotten that the yard of this particular institution was too small to accommodate all the inmates at one time. They could, of course, have ordered all the inmates back into their cells and brought them into the yard in smaller numbers at a time for "processing" and transfer to the trucks. That would have been the most logical procedure. But for some reason the SS men did not do that. Instead, they attempted to ease the crush in the yard by leading long columns of prisoners away from the yard, not back into the prison building but out into the open streets, where reserve trucks had been waiting.

I am not a particularly religious man, but the confusion which resulted from this sudden change in proceedings seemed to me a hint from God that I must take charge of my own fate. This might well be my last opportunity to make a bid for freedom, even for survival. I now felt I owed it to Pela and our baby at least to make an effort to escape. All these thoughts, of course, came to me within split seconds, and I acted quickly. One of the circumstances that influenced my decision was that I still wore the clothes in which I had been arrested. Neither I nor my fellow inmates had been given prison uniforms. As a consequence, neither the Germans nor the Polish police who were standing by noticed me when I made my way out of the jostling crowd of prisoners and quickly ducked into a side street.

Pela and my father were speechless with amazement when they opened our apartment door to find me standing there, filthy, unshaven but very much alive.

However, this was no time for an emotional family reunion. I was sure that the Germans, after the initial confusion of the disorganized exodus from Gesia Street, would check their inmate list and comb the ghetto for Jews who had escaped. I therefore did not stay in our apartment but for the next few days took up residence in the attic of our building where I did not expect the Gestapo to look so soon.

I slept very little during that first night of freedom. My mind was now focused on only one thought: that the one way in which I could give my family, and myself, a chance to survive was by escaping from the ghetto. We would have to pose as Polish Christians and live either in the city's "Aryan sector" or in the Polish countryside (preferably the latter) until Hitler and his Reich would go down in defeat.

9

The reports which spread through the Warsaw ghetto with lightning speed during the days that followed my abrupt departure from the Gesia Street prison only confirmed me in my resolve to escape from the Warsaw ghetto with my family.

On July 23, the day following the start of the mass deportation, Adam Czerniakow, the chairman of Warsaw's *Judenrat*, committed suicide. He had received orders from the occupation authorities to have his *Ordnungsdienst* round up Jews who had not reported for "resettlement" on their own accord. The night preceding the deportation, Czerniakov had been seen riding in a rickshaw through the streets of the ghetto, stopping here and there, appealing to the Jews not to lose their courage and assuring them that ample food, shelter and employment were awaiting them in the labor camps. In fact, of course, Czerniakow, more than any other Jew in the Warsaw ghetto, was in a position to know the fate which awaited the Jews of Warsaw, and he found that he could not go on living with the knowledge that he would be instrumental in sending thousands of his fellow Jews to their death. The next day he took poison. According to those who last saw him alive, his final words were that all the other Jews in the Warsaw ghetto should follow his example and thereby avoid the agony and torture of the "resettlement" the Germans had in mind.

I did not feel like following the example set by Adam Czerniakow, or like waiting passively until the Germans would come for us. Already, the Germans had informed the *Judenrat* that they expected the *Ordnungsdienst* to produce six to ten thousand Jews each day for "resettlement." At the same time, after more mature thought, I realized that our escape from the ghetto required careful preparations. The question was how we could evade deportation until the time that we were ready to escape from the ghetto with a reasonable chance of success.

Once more, luck was with us. The occupation authorities announced that Jews who were employed by the *Judenrat* or by the *Ordnungsdienst*, or who had been assigned to work for German war or other "essential" industries outside the ghetto, would be exempt from deportation, and that this immunity would extend also to their immediate families who were part of their households. These privileged individuals would be given special work permits which they had to carry with them at all times and which the German authorities would honor. Through a friend of mine who had connections with the Polish underground I succeeded in obtaining "homemade" (read "forged") work permits for myself, Pela, my father and Pela's parents.

Meanwhile, the killing and the dying continued in the Warsaw ghetto. In addition to the daily "quotas" of Jews delivered by the *Judenrat* to the Germans for deportation, the Germans still rounded up smaller groups of Jews in the streets and loaded them onto trucks for the journey to the death camps.

One day my mother's oldest sister—the one whose husband had dropped dead while reaching for the roll Pela had intended for her—knocked on our door. She was barely able to stand, much less walk, but she had come to us as a last resort. "Help me find my son!" she sobbed. It seemed that one of her two sons, a boy of 12, had left home and had not returned at the time he had promised to be back. She was frantic; she feared that he had been

101

picked up in the street by the Germans. Armed with my work permit to protect myself from being seized, I spent most of that day searching the streets of the ghetto for the boy, but I never found him.

His mother had good reason to fear for her son's life because the Germans were now also killing children in the streets. One day, as I left my apartment building, I saw a small body lying on the sidewalk in front of the house. It was a boy, hardly more than five or six years old. His features were no longer recognizable because his head had been smashed. A woman, his mother, squatted on the ground beside him, tearing at her hair and whimpering. I tried to raise her from the ground but she refused to budge. "If you want to do me a favor," she said, "please kill me, because I am not brave enough to do it myself."

By the last week in July, the Germans started attempts to flush out the Jews who were hiding in the attics and cellars of apartment buildings to escape deportation. One of the things the Germans seemed to fear was cellars. Perhaps they were afraid that the Jews had turned their basements into underground fortifications. At any rate, the same SS men who bravely broke into apartments to drag out Jews refused to search for them in the cellars. And so the Gestapo devised a new way of picking off the Jews in the cellars: the Germans did not enter the cellars themselves but trained their machine guns at cellar doors and windows, and riddled them with bullets. In this way they were able to kill the Jews hidden inside without any risk of harm to themselves. It was clear to me that soon no Jew in the Warsaw ghetto would be safe from deportation. I was not even sure that a work permit, faked or real, would afford protection for long. And so I was all the more determined to complete my preparations for our escape from the ghetto as soon as possible.

The most important prerequisite for our escape was a set of documents proving that we were "Aryans." I made arrangements to obtain "Aryan" papers through my friend Edward Galewski, who, along with his wife (they had no children), planned to escape from the ghetto together with us. Before the war, Edward and his brother Oskar had been in the lumber business, in which they had associated mostly with Gentiles. Oskar had managed to stay outside the ghetto and lived as an "Aryan" in the "Aryan sector." A widower with an eight-year-old daughter, Oskar had been able to pass as a Polish Gentile not only thanks to his "Aryan" surname (which had been his by birth) and his "Aryan" documents (which were forged) but also because his fair hair and blue eyes made him look every inch a Pole and it would never have occurred to anyone that Oskar Galewski might be a Jew. Oskar had become active in the Polish underground, and it was through his underground connections that he had been able to order homemade "Aryan" documents not only for his brother Edward and for his wife, but also for Pela and myself.

I received word from Edward to meet him at a certain hour one afternoon on Swietoyerska Street. I knew this meant that Edward had received our "Aryan" papers and would hand them over to me. On the date agreed upon, I set out to keep my appointment with Edward but, as things turned out, I was to be unavoidably detained.

As I walked toward Swietoyerska Street to meet Edward, I saw SS men on motorcycles, followed by several German army trucks, converging on the area. This was what the Germans called a "street blockade." The SS, without warning, surrounded a number of blocks in order to arrest all the Jews who lived there. I knew that if

I got caught in this "blockade," I would not be able to avoid arrest.

I therefore turned off into the nearest side street, Nalewki, where I took cover behind the entrance of an apartment building. From this vantage point I had a clear view of the scene. I watched as a German army truck pulled up at the next corner and discharged a crew of SS men who started seizing Jews in the street at random. Working alongside the SS troopers were members of the *Judenrat's Ordnungsdienst*. I saw one of the Jewish policemen grab an elderly woman and, to my horror, realized that she was Mrs. Grubstein, one of my mother's closest friends. Short and stout, she attempted to escape, but she could not run away fast enough and the policeman was about to shove her onto the army truck. I could not stand by idly while my mother's friend was in danger. I rushed out from behind the gateway where I had been hiding, ran toward the Jewish policemen and, yelling Polish curses at them, leaped onto the truck, grabbed Mrs. Grubstein and jumped off the truck again, dragging the old lady with me.

As I hit the ground, my legs buckled under me and I felt a sharp pain in my abdomen. For some moments, I could not straighten my body. Luckily, the Germans seemed unaware of Mrs. Grubstein's escape, for the truck, crammed with Jews, drove off, leaving Mrs. Grubstein and me behind. A couple of *Ordnungsdienst* men were standing nearby with a stunned, sheepish look on their faces. I signaled to one of them to take Mrs. Grubstein to a safe place, but Mrs. Grubstein refused to leave me because she realized that I had been hurt. She hailed a passing rickshaw and, together with two of the Jewish policemen, hoisted me into it. I knew that I was in no condition to keep my appointment with Edward Galewski and gave the rickshaw man my home address.

I must give credit to the *Ordnungsdienst* men who came to our rescue. Although the street blockade had ended as abruptly as it had begun, these Jewish fellows risked their lives by helping Mrs. Grubstein and me.

When the rickshaw stopped in front of my apartment building, I found that I could not stand up. I felt a searing pain as if something were tearing inside my abdomen. The driver carefully lifted me from the rickshaw, then supported me as we slowly made our way to the house. Pela, who had been sitting by the window, had seen me arrive. When she saw me bent over double, leaning heavily upon the rickshaw driver, her first thought was that I had been hit by a bullet. It was obvious to me that I would not be able to walk up the steps to our apartment on the third floor. So I asked the rickshaw driver to help me to the apartment of a neighbor on the ground floor. By that time Pela was at my side. She took one look at me and immediately went for a doctor. (There still were a few doctors left in the ghetto.)

The doctor came, examined me and diagnosed a hernia, a result of my flying leap from the German truck with Mrs. Grubstein. Of course, there could be no thought of operating on me now. But luckily there still was one trussmaker in the ghetto who made a rupture belt for me.

I remained in bed at the neighbor's apartment for two days. Then I put on the belt and resumed my preparations for our escape.

On 30 Swietoyerska Street there was a warehouse owned by a small chemical plant located in the "Aryan sector." This factory, which apparently was doing some work essential to the German war effort, employed Jews in the ghetto to make wooden delivery crates for their products. Trucks would enter the ghetto to pick up the cases and take them to the plant in the "Aryan sector."

One of the truck drivers who regularly made the trip to the ghetto was known to be friendly toward Jews, particularly if he could get a cash reward for it. I made a deal with him whereby I would be allowed to fill up a few empty delivery crates with clothes and small household articles we would need for our new life outside the ghetto. I also added a few things that belonged to Edward Galewski. Edward's brother Oskar then went to the plant to pick up the contents of the crates, which he took to his apartment in the "Aryan sector" to keep until Edward and we would turn up.

I went to Edward's apartment, apologized for not having kept my original appointment with him, and received the "Aryan" papers which his brother Oskar had sent through his underground connections for Pela and myself. I was now no longer Adam Starkopf, a Jew born and raised in Warsaw, but Adam Bludowski, a pure "Aryan" born in Kazan, Russia. Pela became Zofia Bludowski. She, too, had been turned into a native of Russia; according to her new papers, she had been born in Leningrad. The reason for the Russian birthplaces was that, since Germany was now at war with the Soviet Union, the Germans would not be able to check the authenticity of our birth certificates.

Originally, of course, my plan had been that my father and Pela's parents should leave the ghetto together with us. But on second thought this did not seem wise to me. It would be foolhardy, I told myself, to subject three people, all of them past middle age, to the dangers of an escape from the ghetto without even knowing where and how we would find shelter for them. Pela and I did not look Jewish and so would have no difficulty passing as "Aryans" and finding a place to live, even without our forged documents. My father and Pela's parents, on the other hand, could be identified as Jews at first sight.

"Aryan" papers alone would not be enough to protect them. They would therefore not be able to live "in the open," but would have to go into hiding, probably on some Polish farmstead. This in turn entailed the problem of finding a decent, reliable peasant who would not give them away to the Germans at the first opportunity.

I concluded that Pela, the baby and I should go first, find a room or apartment for ourselves, and then try to seek out "Aryans" who could be trusted to help us find a safe hiding place for our parents. Once we had secured a hideout for our parents we would arrange to have them smuggled out of the ghetto to join us. My father and Pela's parents still had the work permits I had gotten for them. I had to take the chance that these papers would protect them from deportation for a few more days until Pela and I could safely send for them.

It was very difficult for me to persuade Pela to leave her parents and my father alone in the ghetto. Most of our other relatives had died or had been deported. My father's brother David, who had been a wealthy business-man before the war, had died in the ghetto of starvation. Two other brothers—Uncle Maurice with his wife and fourteen-year-old daughter, and Uncle Nuciek with his wife and their daughter of seventeen—had gone to Tre-blinka. So had my father's two sisters—Helen with her husband and two daughters, twenty and sixteen, and Maria with her husband. My mother's sister Stefa and her husband had been shot in their apartment together with their beloved pet dog. My mother's oldest sister had died of starvation without ever finding out what had become of her son. Pela's mother had been one of five sisters. All her four sisters, along with their husbands and children, had gone to Treblinka. Pela's grandmother, who had lived with the oldest sister, had lost her life on the day of the first German *Aktion*; she had been among those elderly Jews who had been shot in the Jewish cemetery and buried in a mass grave.

One of Pela's cousins, a boy of 14, was found in the street, dead, his body cut and bruised. A neighbor told us what had happened to him. The Germans had caught him, tied him to the tail of an army truck and dragged him for several blocks. When they presumed he must be dead, they had cut him loose and left him lying in the middle of the street.

Our apprehensions about leaving my father and Pela's parents were eased by good news from Edward Galewski. His brother Oskar had decided that the best place for us to live would be the town of Lochow, about 100 miles east of Warsaw on the railroad line between Warsaw and Bialystok. We would certainly be safe there with our "Aryan" looks and papers, Edward assured us, because even Jews who did not look "Aryan" and had no "Aryan" papers, including some relatives of the Galewskis, were living in Lochow unmolested. These relatives had found a hideout for my father and my parents-in-law in a little village not far from Lochow, where a Polish peasant had agreed to give them shelter under the floor of his barn. They would have to remain hidden there all day long. Admittedly, this hideout would not afford them much light or air, but at night a trapdoor in the floor would be raised and our parents would be able to catch a little air at least for a few hours after dark each night. We, who would be living "in the open" as "Aryans," would have frequent opportunities to visit them from Lochow and to bring them food.

Pela and I were happy that at least a temporary solution had been found for our parents. We were confident now that they would be able to join us in a matter of days after our own departure, and so we prepared to leave Warsaw, if one can describe our feelings in such terms,

108

with a lighter heart than we might have done otherwise.

In order to explain the manner in which Pela, Jasia and I—along with Edward Galewski and his wife—escaped from the Warsaw ghetto by the way of the Jewish cemetery, I must describe in some detail the "geography" of the area through which we had to travel.

The Warsaw ghetto, as I have already mentioned earlier in my story, was surrounded by a brick wall, broken at 14 points by gates which were constantly guarded by SS men and police. The Jewish cemetery, as I have also pointed out earlier, was outside the area set aside for the ghetto. It bordered the west side of Okopowa Street, a thoroughfare which ran approximately north and south, parallel with part of the ghetto's wall. Gesia Street, one of the main east-west arteries of the ghetto, terminated on the east side of Okopowa. At the point where Gesia and Okopowa Streets met, there was one of the 14 ghetto gates. Directly across Okopowa Street from this gate, on the west side of Okopowa, was the entrance to the Jewish cemetery. North and south of this crossing point the Germans had mounted devices which could be raised and lowered like railroad crossing barriers to block off Okopowa Street and form a narrow, closed corridor between the ghetto and the Jewish cemetery. When a Jewish funeral procession left the ghetto for the cemetery through the Gesia Street gate, these barriers would be lowered, allowing the mourners to cross the street from the ghetto to the cemetery and back but making it impossible for them to escape from the ghetto by turning either right or left on Okopowa Street. Polish vehicles and pedestrians on Okopowa Street had to stop and wait until the Jewish funeral procession had crossed the street and the barriers had been raised again.

Adjoining the Jewish cemetery on the west, and separated from the latter by walls and other partitions, were a Catholic cemetery and an old Tartar burial ground. Aware that Jews seeking to escape from the ghetto by way of the Jewish cemetery might attempt to pass into the "Aryan sector" through these burial grounds, the Germans guarded the gates of each cemetery with special care.

After the first mass deportation of July, 1942, Jewish families were no longer permitted to accompany their dead from the ghetto into the Jewish cemetery. Instead, cemetery employees would be sent into the ghetto to pick up the dead from the place where they had died—their homes, the hospital, or the street—and to transport them in pushcarts to the cemetery, where other workers saw to their burial. Often, many bodies would be buried together in one grave. The families in most cases never learned the location of the site where their loved ones were buried.

There was now only one way in which we would be able to escape from the ghetto with an infant who could not be counted upon to remain quiet. We would have to pretend that our baby was dead, and we would have to bribe the ghetto guards to let us out so that we, the distraught parents, could be present at the cemetery when she was buried. From the cemetery we would then make our way into the "Aryan sector."

When I revealed this plan to my father and to Pela's parents, they were horrified. It was insane, they said, to take such chances with Pela and the baby. They begged our neighbors and friends to talk us out of our madness. One of my neighbors tried to impress upon me that instead of exposing my family to the perils of the unknown I should concentrate on obtaining a legitimate work permit in place of the forged one which I had been carrying. I should get a real job in one of the German-run ghetto workshops which produced uniforms and other articles for the German army. Once I had a job in such a place, I could be certain that the Germans would not deport me and my family, and I would not be risking the lives of my wife and child.

But I would not listen. I felt I would not have peace unless I went through with my plan.

I set the date for our escape: July 31, 1942. The night before, none of us slept. I sat by the crib in which Jasia was sleeping peacefully. As I looked at her, I was plagued by doubts which, until then, I had somehow been able to suppress. Perhaps our parents and friends were right, after all. Did I have the right to risk the life of my child? Even if we escaped without being caught, what assurance did I have that I would be able to keep Jasia alive? How could I be certain that she would not get sick, or starve? Would our escape really give her a chance to survive the war and to grow to maturity, or would it only bring her prolonged agony ending in a horrible death?

All night long my father and Pela's parents begged me to reconsider. I put the choice to Pela, going over with her once again the possible benefits and all the probable risks of escaping from the ghetto and of attempting to pass as "Aryans" with a small child. This time Pela took my side against our parents. In fact, she declared that she would prefer to take the leap now, rather than put off our escape and perhaps blame herself forever after for having deprived me and our child of the opportunity to survive. We had to escape now, she said, if for no other reason but that the Galewski brothers' relatives in Lochow had already found a hiding place for her parents and my father, so that we would be able to bring our parents to safety almost immediately after our own arrival on the "Aryan side." I had made arrangements with a distant relative, whose name was Michael and who was working in the Jewish cemetery, to help smuggle our parents out of the ghetto.

Little did I know then that only a few days after our escape it would be too late for our parents to follow us.

Early in the afternoon of July 31, 1942, Pela and I bade our parents farewell. We both tried very hard to suppress our hidden fear that, despite all our careful planning for them and for ourselves, it was possible that we might never see them again. I forced myself to think only of the indignities and the cruelties to which I would be exposing my wife and my baby daughter if we would stay on in the ghetto. This thought alone gave me the strength to part from my own father without a show of emotion and to help Pela through the ordeal of leaving her father and mother.

Several hours earlier I had taken Jasia to the apartment of friends on Novolipki 43 so that our parents, in our own apartment, would not see what we would have to do with Jasia in preparation for our escape.

When we arrived at our friends' apartment after leaving our parents, another friend, a doctor, was already waiting for us there with his medical bag. He took out a syringe and gave Jasia an injection to put her to sleep. "This should keep her sleeping for about half an hour, perhaps even for three-quarters of an hour, just long enough to get you inside the cemetery," the doctor said.

The plan for our escape was as follows: At 1:30 in the afternoon, Pela and the baby would leave from Novolipki 43, in a covered hearse, for the cemetery. Jasia would be in the hearse, in a casket. Pela, dressed in deep mourning, would follow the hearse. The hearse would arrive at the ghetto gate on Okopowa Street, directly opposite the entrance to the cemetery, at 1:45 sharp, fifteen minutes before the guard whom we had bribed to let us out would go off duty. In order not to attract undue attention, I would arrive on foot at Okopowa Street by a different route and station myself inside the ghetto, some distance away from the gate, to watch while the hearse carrying Pela and Jasia crossed Okopowa Street into the cemetery. The hearse would proceed to the morgue inside the cemetery where the dead were prepared for burial. Pela and Jasia would go inside and wait for me there to pick them up at about nine o'clock that evening, well after dark.

After I had seen Pela and Jasia enter the cemetery safely, I would return to our apartment to tell Pela's parents that their daughter and granddaughter had completed the first stage of our journey, and to meet Edward Galewski and his wife, who had agreed to wait for me at the apartment. Then, the Galewskis and I would leave the ghetto, not through the Jewish cemetery but through a hole in an inconspicuous, unguarded part of the ghetto wall. Once in the "Aryan sector," we would head for the Tartar cemetery. From there, that night, I would climb over the wall into the Jewish cemetery. With the help of the caretaker of the Tartar burial ground, a Mr. Navoyak, I would assist my wife and baby over the wall into the Tartar cemetery. From there, the three of us, joined by the Galewskis, would proceed directly to the exit, out into Mlynarska Street, in the "Aryan sector." Since there would be no train to Lochow until late the next evening, we would have to spend the night in the "Aryan sector" of Warsaw. Oskar had sent word to Edward that he had found a room for us, for one night, in an apartment on Jerozolimska Avenue, directly opposite the city's main railroad terminal.

Neither Pela nor I will ever forget our exodus from the Warsaw ghetto. Our departure from Novolipki 43 was strictly on schedule. The horse-drawn cart I had hired pulled up in front of the building at 1:25 sharp. The driver opened the door of his hearse and took out a small, rectangular wooden box, which he brought into the apartment of my friends. The box had no lid; it was covered only with a black cloth. This was to be Jasia's casket. It had already done duty countless times in the burial of babies who had died in the ghetto. The casket was used only to take the body to the cemetery. In the cemetery, the baby would be lifted out of the casket and placed into the grave wrapped only in a bedsheet. Then the casket would be ready for the next funeral.

Jasia was already sound asleep. I carefully wrapped her into an old bed sheet and gently placed her into the casket, which I then covered again with its black cloth. Meanwhile, Pela changed into an old black dress her friend had lent her, and put on a black hat over which she draped a black veil to conceal her face. Then the driver picked up the little casket, with Jasia in it, and carried it down the steps. Pela and I followed him.

The driver placed the casket into his hearse, and then climbed into the driver's seat. Pela followed the hearse on foot.

At 1:30 sharp I signaled the driver to start out. After the cart had moved some distance away, I set out on my own route to Okopowa Street.

It was vital that the cart bearing Jasia should arrive at the Jewish cemetery no later, but also no earlier, than 1:45 P.M., fifteen minutes before the guard changed at the Gesia Street gate of the ghetto. No later, because at 2 o'clock sharp the SS guard and his companion from the Polish police, whom we had given a gift of food and cash to let the cart pass through the ghetto gate, would be relieved by two other guards whom we had not bribed and whom we did not know. But also no earlier, because of the rule that all permits given to Jews to visit the cemetery expired after 15 minutes. If the holder of such a permit stayed in the cemetery beyond that deadline, the guards would enter the cemetery to look for him. But if

114

the end of our allotted quarter-hour coincided with the changing of the guards at 2 o'clock the old guards would no longer be responsible for us and the new guards who took their place would not know that Pela was in the cemetery. She would then be able to wait unmolested until I would come for her that evening. As far as the guards knew, Pela was the only one to be allowed to see her child buried, since Jewish families were no longer permitted to escort their dead to the cemetery.

When I arrived at the Gesia Street gate, the hearse had just passed through the gate and was crossing Okopowa Street. I remained standing several yards from the gate and watched as the hearse creaked toward the entrance to the Jewish cemetery. I saw an SS man signal the driver of the hearse to stop. I did not know this man. "*Auf-machen!* (Open that!)" the SS man shouted at the driver, pointing to the door of the hearse. The driver jumped from his seat and opened the door. I saw that the SS man was wearing gloves; I remember they were gray. My breath stopped as he bent over Jasia's casket. "That's no real funeral," I could hear the driver telling the German. "It's just a dead baby. Poor thing—it had typhoid fever." I saw the SS man slam the door of the hearse, turn on his heel and walk off swiftly. The mere word "typhoid fever" was sufficient to frighten even an SS man.

The hearse moved on. I breathed more easily. The first stage of our escape had been completed. I turned away from the ghetto gate and walked back to our apartment to report the news to my father and Pela's parents.

However, as I later learned, Pela had one more close call. As the hearse entered the cemetery, a cemetery worker opened the door of the hearse. "You're really not supposed to be here," he told Pela. "I'll take the child and bury it." He pointed his finger to an open mass grave not far away. Pela began to scream, "Don't touch her! She's alive!" The man's mouth flew open in disbelief. The hearse moved on.

The hearse's next stop was at the little morgue where the cemetery employees prepared the bodies for burial. Once again, an attendant offered to bury Jasia. The driver of the hearse whispered something in his ear. The attendant's mouth opened again in amazement; he turned aside and allowed Pela to enter the building with Jasia.

Pela sat down on a wooden bench inside this morgue, surrounded by dead bodies and sickened by the stench of decay. At her feet, in the casket, lay Jasia, fast asleep. But after a while, Jasia's eyes opened ever so slightly. Pela feared that the effects of the injection the doctor had given Jasia were beginning to wear off. Pela bent over the casket, lifted Jasia out and rocked her in her arms, praying that if Jasia awoke, she would be able to keep her quiet for the next seven hours, until I would arrive. Pela had hidden under her dress a small bottle of milk and some food for Jasia.

In the meantime, I entered our apartment. There I found Edward Galewski and his wife already waiting for me. The time had come for me to bid farewell to my father and to Pela's parents. In order to make it as easy for them as possible, I kept our parting deliberately casual, as if I fully expected to see them again the next day, or the day after, at the latest.

In the evening, Edward, his wife and I left the ghetto through an unguarded hole in the wall. Minutes later, the three of us were in the "Aryan sector." We ripped off our Jewish armbands and passed into the Tartar cemetery through its main entrance. From there, shortly before nine o'clock, I climbed over the partition into the Jewish cemetery and went to the building where Pela was waiting for me. Jasia was still half asleep, a little pale but, much to my relief, not looking as if the injection had harmed her.

Pela handed Jasia to me. I took the baby into my arms and, together, we walked toward one of the old family mausoleums in the center of the cemetery. We hid inside this mausoleum until 9:30. Then we moved soundlessly toward the wall, twelve feet high, which separated the Jewish cemetery from the Tartar burial ground. Directly adjoining that wall, on the Tartar side, was the hut in which Mr. Navoyak, the caretaker, lived with his wife.

I handed Jasia back to Pela and left the two standing behind one massive tombstone not far from the wall. I went to the wall and picked up a rock, with which I knocked on the wall three times. This was my signal to Mr. Navoyak. Then I moved a few paces away and lay down flat on my back behind one of the tombstones from where I could see the top of the wall without the danger of anyone seeing me.

A few minutes later I heard the sound of swift steps climbing a stepladder on the other side of the wall. Next, I saw Mr. Navoyak's head appear above the top of the wall. I went toward him.

"Edward and his wife are already at my house," Navoyak whispered, mouthing the words carefully so I could read his lips.

"How are things on Mlynarska Street?" I whispered back. "Everything quiet?"

Navoyak vanished behind the wall. After a while his head reappeared. He nodded to me. He pushed a step-ladder over the top of the wall. I caught it and leaned it against our side of the wall. We had to move swiftly and very quietly because the Gestapo patrols sometimes made spot checks of the wall between the two cemeteries during the night. I helped Pela climb the first rung of the ladder. She climbed the rest of the way unaided. I followed her, carrying Jasia in the crook of my right arm.

117

Miraculously, the child was still not awake. When we reached the top of the wall, Mr. Navoyak quickly climbed down the stepladder on which he had been standing so that Pela, and then I, could descend on it into the Tartar burial ground.

As soon as our feet touched the ground on his side, Mr. Navoyak raced back up the ladder and reached over the wall to withdraw the other ladder, which still leaned against the Jewish side. Holding this ladder in his left arm, he came down again, then hid both ladders behind some bushes. He accomplished all this virtually without a sound.

Meanwhile Pela and I—Pela was now holding Jasia again—ran into Mr. Navoyak's cottage, where the Galewskis were waiting for us.

Edward and I instructed our wives to walk slowly, very slowly, ahead of us toward the exit of the cemetery which was on Mlynarska Street. On Mlynarska Street, close to this exit, there was a streetcar stop. We would take the next car that went to Jerozolimska Avenue. Edward and I followed our wives at some distance. Still not a sound from Jasia.

Almost as soon as the two women reached the stop, a streetcar arrived. It was the one we wanted. The women climbed aboard. Edward and I quickened our steps to catch up with them but waited until the bell sounded to signal that the car was leaving before we ourselves jumped onto the rear platform of the car. There were only a few other passengers.

We were careful not to take seats too close together. We pretended not to know each other. A group of four people, with a baby, traveling together at this late hour, would attract too much attention.

The streetcar bell clanged once more and the car pulled away from the stop. I furtively looked out the window as the wall of the Tartar cemetery receded into the distance. For better or for worse, we had left the Warsaw ghetto behind us.

10

When we arrived at the apartment building on Jerozolimska Avenue, Edward's brother Oskar was waiting inside the entryway. He took us to the room he had found for us in an apartment on the seventh floor. The owner of the apartment, an artist, was active in the Polish underground. Ironically, this apartment building housed also the headquarters of the German Railroad Police. This was precisely why Oskar Galewski had chosen it for our overnight stop in Warsaw's "Aryan sector." He felt we would be safer there than anywhere else, because no one would think of hunting for Jews in a building that contained an official German agency. I later learned that this apartment had already sheltered many members of the Polish underground, but no Jews. This night, however, we were the only fugitives there.

The artist's wife had prepared us something to eat. We thanked her politely but took nothing. We were not very hungry, we said. The truth was that we could have done with some food, but we were afraid that if we acted too hungry, the lady might suspect that we were not members of the Polish underground, as Oskar had made her believe, but Jews who had just escaped from months of starvation in the ghetto. We did not know how the artist and his wife felt about Jews. Many members of the Polish underground had even less love for Jews than they had for the Germans.

Neither Edward nor I slept much that night. We spent the hours planning for our immediate future—our lives as Polish "Aryans" in the town of Lochow.

From time to time I looked in the direction of the mattress which Edward's wife, Pela and Jasia shared. Jasia was still sleeping off the injection she had received in the ghetto.

The next morning our hostess handed me a copy of *Rzeczpospolita*, a mimeographed secret bulletin put out by the Polish underground. This bulletin, I later found out, was the first to tell the truth about Treblinka. I had suspected all along that, contrary to what the Germans had tried to make the Jews believe, Treblinka was not a labor camp but a death camp. Now I saw my fears confirmed by a detailed account in the Polish underground bulletin. As I read the page of faint mimeograph print, I shuddered. Time was running out for my father, for Pela's parents and for all the other Jews who were still in the Warsaw ghetto.

The next train for Lochow was not due to leave until late in the evening. We spent the entire day in the apartment, afraid to venture out into the street before dark. Jasia was herself again, wide awake but, to our delight, quiet and seemingly undisturbed by the change in her environment.

At nine o'clock in the evening we left the apartment building and crossed the street to the railroad terminal. Now at last I understood how a fugitive from the police must feel. All around me people were milling about, free to travel wherever they chose, while I was in fear for my own life and for the lives of my wife and child. I had heard that German policemen were patrolling the station, closely watching the crowds in the terminal for faces that looked Jewish.

When our train pulled in, we boarded it, careful again not to sit together. The lights in the cars were out because the electricity in all civilian railroad cars had been shut off. But under the circumstances we considered this a

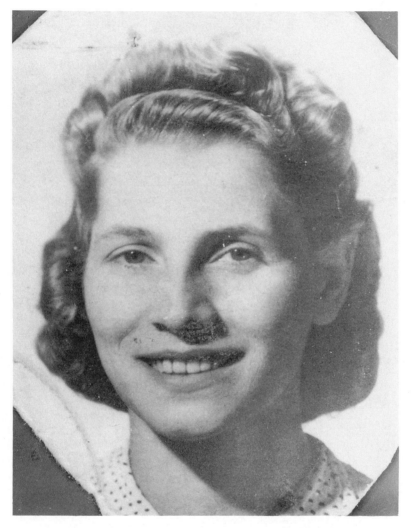

Pela. Picture taken on the "Aryan" side for her forged identity card *(Kennkarte)*. According to regulations, the left ear had to be exposed, as in photographs taken of criminals.

stroke of good fortune because no one in the car would be able to look at our faces.

We arrived in Lochow at midnight. Lochow was one of the very few towns in the German sector of Poland where Jews still lived in relative peace. We had heard that the German commandant of the town was quite humane as Germans went. The Jews of Lochow had organized a committee which kept collecting funds and gifts to cultivate the commandant's good will. In return, so the story went, the commandant had assured the Jews of Lochow that they would not be deported. In the event that he would receive orders to hand the Jews over for deportation, he had said, he would give the Jews advance warning so they could make arrangements to escape in time. Each Jewish family had one bag packed, ready to flee at a moment's notice. The Jews of Lochow did not seem to understand that once the Gestapo decided to go into action, it would be as good as impossible for them to escape.

We went directly to the Galewskis' relatives, who lived in a spacious house. They agreed to take us in until we could find more permanent quarters. While Edward's wife, Pela and Jasia rested there, Edward, Oskar and I began our search for a new home. To forestall questions about our being "new in town," we explained to prospective landlords that the three of us had jobs in a large lumberyard near Lochow and were now looking for a "summer place" in which to spend the vacation months.

Two days after our arrival in Lochow I had found a place for Pela, Jasia and myself in the village of Zambrzyniec, about 12 miles outside Lochow. It was one room, with a stove, in the cottage of a peasant woman, Mrs. Slovik. Compared to the other Polish peasants in the area, Mrs. Slovik, a widow, was fairly well off: she owned several acres of land, three cows, a few pigs, one horse and one wagon. But her farm was very much neglected because her grown sons, who should have helped her manage the place, were constantly in trouble with the police. They always seemed to be involved in knife fights or in drunken brawls. They secretly manufactured, in their mother's cellar, a kind of cheap vodka made from potatoes and corn, but instead of allowing their mother to sell it for some extra money she so badly needed, they drank it all themselves.

Mrs. Slovik's house was unbelievably filthy, and so was Mrs. Slovik herself. She proudly told us that she had not washed her hair since her wedding day, thirty-five years earlier. Every Sunday morning, after church, one of her granddaughters would come to her room, sit down beside her on a low stool, and pick the lice from her grandmother's greasy grey hair.

It was to the home of this fine family that Pela, Jasia and I moved on August 4, 1942. Edward Galewski and his wife found a small place not far away.

On August 5, after settling our wives and Jasia in their new homes, Edward, Oskar and I returned to Warsaw to make arrangements for taking my father and Pela's parents out of the ghetto. At nine o'clock that evening I entered the Jewish cemetery from the Tartar burial ground to meet my relative, Michael, who had agreed to smuggle my father, Pela's parents and his own wife out of the ghetto by way of the cemetery.

I lay down on the ground between two monuments, waiting for Michael to appear. It was a very dark night. Once in a while I heard voices and strange sounds from among the graves nearby. These were Polish hoodlums who came to the Jewish cemetery at night, dug up the dead and pulled the gold teeth from their mouths. Since most of the recent dead in the Jewish cemetery had been buried without caskets, this task was not too difficult. It was no pleasure for me to be in such company but I was not afraid. If they noticed me and tried to start trouble, I would be able to handle them easily, I told myself. After all, they were not Gestapo men with machine guns.

At 10:30 P.M. Michael appeared. We shook hands. "Everything's ready," he said. He instructed me not to come with him into the ghetto but to wait in the cemetery for my family. He explained that he was about to drive a horse-drawn burial wagon into the ghetto to pick up the dead. My father, Pela's parents and Michael's wife would board this wagon and be smuggled into the Jewish cemetery with a carload of corpses.

I was so sure everything would go well that I urged Michael to bring out his sister as well. "I'll find a place for her in Lochow, too," I promised.

"Don't worry, Adam. Just wait here. I'll be back with everybody before you know it," said Michael, and disappeared.

A little later, I heard several bursts of gunfire, but I did not move from my hiding place. Shooting in the ghetto had become such a common occurrence that one hardly paid attention to it anymore.

One hour passed, then two hours, without a sign of Michael. The church bells struck midnight, then one o'clock in the morning. A shadow was moving toward me, then crouched on the ground beside me. It was one of the cemetery employees. He was out of breath and even in the darkness I could see the horror in his face.

"Didn't you hear the shooting?" he gasped. "This isn't just another little German raid. It's a mass killing operation. Michael and his wife—they were on the way back here, but they never made it. The Germans caught them with the wagon. Michael is dead. So is his wife." He did not seem to know that, in addition to Michael and his wife, the burial wagon should have contained three other living persons.

I felt the blood drain from my face. "I'm going back to the ghetto," I whispered. "My father—my wife's parents..."

"You must be out of your mind," the man hissed. "There's nothing you can do for anybody inside the ghetto now. Get out of here. Back to the 'Aryan' sector, to your wife and child. Think of them. What'll become of them if the Germans kill you too?"

It was a sensible argument but I was in no mood to accept it now. I followed him into the little morgue from where, only a few days earlier, I had taken Pela and Jasia to freedom. In front of the morgue, cemetery employees were harnessing wagons. They were leaving for the ghetto to pick up bodies. Apparently the Germans had left many dead in the streets of the ghetto, and the Gestapo, with their usual efficiency, had sent word to the cemetery to have the bodies removed at once.

I entered the morgue in the cemetery. Inside, I found a pair of tattered overalls which obviously had been discarded by one of the workers. I took off my own clothes and put on the overalls. Then I leaped onto the driver's seat of one of the wagons and sat down beside the driver. In my rags, I could have been the driver's helper. This was how I returned to the ghetto to look for my father and my wife's parents.

Inside the ghetto, I jumped off the wagon at the corner of Gesia and Smocza Streets. All seemed quiet there. Hugging the walls of the buildings, I walked swiftly toward Novolipki Street. As I approached Novolipki, the quiet was broken by bursts of gunfire, and by screams interspersed with raucous shouts in German. I was afraid that my knees would give way under me, but I broke into a run. My father and Pela's parents needed me. But when I arrived at the corner of Novolipki Street, I found my way blocked by German army trucks and motorcycles. I had come within sight of our apartment building but I was unable to move any closer.

I hid in the doorway of a bombed-out house near the corner of Novolipki. After a while the German trucks and motorcycles began to move away in a long column. The trucks were filled with Jews—men, women and children—but I could not distinguish their faces in the dark. For a moment I was tempted to jump aboard the next truck that would pass. Perhaps my father was in one of the trucks. Perhaps, by some miracle, I would be able to find him and to save him! Or Pela's parents! But then I remembered that Pela and Jasia were waiting for me in the tiny room in Mrs. Slovik's farmhouse. What would become of them if I did not return? And so I remained standing in the doorway as the long column of trucks, with headlights blazing, passed by.

At last, all was quiet again on Novolipki Street. At dawn, I crept out from behind the doorway and rushed to our apartment building. I ran up the stairs. The front door of our apartment was wide open. I went inside. No one was there. My father and Pela's parents were gone. I sank to the floor and wept for a long, long time.

Hours passed before I could gather the strength to get up and leave the apartment. Outside, I met one of our neighbors. At first I did not recognize him. I knew he was only in his forties, but now his face and gait were those of an old man.

"You...here?" he stammered. "They took your father last night. Your wife's parents, too. They're on their way to Treblinka." He shrugged his shoulders and shook his head. "I'm still here. I wonder why. My turn may come tomorrow." He nodded; then, without another word, he shuffled past me. I could not see, hear or think. If only I had come one day earlier, just one day earlier!

But I could not even mourn now. I had to return to life and to the living. From now on my family consisted only of my wife and our baby, and Pela had only our baby and me. I would do everything in my power to protect them so that we would survive this war together. Without them, life would have no more meaning for me.

"You! Get up here!"

I looked up. The burial wagon on which I had come to the ghetto from the cemetery had stopped in front of me. "I'm going back to the cemetery!" the driver shouted. I was hardly able to move my legs, but I climbed back onto the driver's seat. The wagon was piled high with dead bodies. The streets were now deserted. The Germans had done their day's work.

In the cemetery, I went to the morgue, where I changed back into my own clothes. I stayed inside the morgue until after dark. Then I took a ladder from the morgue and climbed up the wall nearest Mr. Navoyak's hut. By prearrangement with Michael, Mr. Navoyak was supposed to be waiting in his hut for a signal that my father and Pela's parents had arrived in the Jewish cemetery. As I reached the top of the wall, Mr. Navoyak emerged from the hut. Seeing my head above the wall, he ran back into the hut and brought out his own ladder for me to climb down into the Tartar burial ground.

"Where are the others?" Mr. Navoyak asked as I descended the last rung of his ladder.

"You can put your ladder away now, Mr. Navoyak," I managed to mumble. "The others are gone. Deported."

"Then you must not stay here any longer," Mr. Navoyak said. "Go back to your wife and child. Go quickly."

He took his ladder from the wall. Without a word, I pressed his hand and walked toward the gate of the cemetery which led out to Mlynarska Street.

126

11

Dazed, I stumbled through the streets of Warsaw's "Aryan sector" toward the railroad station. How would I be able to tell Pela that her parents were dead? As I turned into Zelazna Street, I heard someone call my name.

"Mister Adam! Adam Starkopf! What are you doing here?" I turned around. Who could know me here? I found myself face to face with Maria Krupka. I remembered her at once. She had been a maid at the house of my friend Jozef, who had studied journalism at the University of Warsaw before the war.

"Perhaps you can help me, Mister Adam," Maria said. "I have Max, Jozef's younger brother, hiding in my apartment. He escaped from the ghetto yesterday. He's badly hurt, but I won't be able to keep him much longer. You see, the apartment is really my sister's, and she's afraid to be caught giving shelter to a Jew."

I remembered Max. He could not be much more than 17 years old, I thought. "Come on, let's walk," Maria said. "Standing at street corners attracts attention."

As we walked down Zelazna Street, Maria Krupka told me the story of Max. It seemed that Max, together with his parents, had been taken to the *Umschlagplatz*, the assembly point in the ghetto where Jews were "processed" for the train journey to Treblinka. Max's parents had already been placed into a long line that was being marched to the waiting boxcars. But Max's group was still waiting near the ghetto wall. Max noticed a hole in the wall. The guard near the hole wore a German uniform, but by his looks Max could tell that he was a Ukrainian. Max carried no baggage, but he had 500 zlotys in his pants pocket. Realizing that he had nothing to lose he strode up to the Ukrainian and pulled out the bills. "Look! Money!" Max said to the guard. "It's all yours if you let me pass through this hole." The guard grabbed the money. "Very good," he said. "Pass." Max climbed through the hole into the "Aryan sector." But then the Ukrainian fired two shots after him, hitting him in the arm. Max was bleeding badly but he had the presence of mind to remember Maria's address. With his good arm, he hailed a rickshaw and told the driver to take him to Towarowa Street.

My heart drew me to Pela and Jasia in Zambrzyniec, but I feared the thought of facing Pela with the news I had to tell her. There were still several hours to go before the next train left Warsaw for Lochow. So I agreed to go with Maria to her sister's apartment. It was on the first floor and had only two rooms. I found Max lying on a sofa. His left shirtsleeve was soaked with blood. His face was pale but there was an unnatural glow in his eyes. Obviously, he was running a fever. He seemed to be in great pain, but he bit his lip to keep from crying out.

When Max saw me, his face brightened. One thing was clear to me at once. Max was in no condition to go anywhere except to a doctor. I remembered a doctor named Alexander, a fine Christian gentleman who had his home and office in the part of Warsaw known as the Old City. I had heard that Dr. Alexander had become active in the Polish underground. I decided he could be trusted to attend to Max without asking questions.

After dark I led Max out of the apartment. He was leaning heavily on my arm. Since I did not want anyone to notice that Max was wounded, I pretended that Max and I were a pair of drunks, looking for a droshky. Our act must have been even more convincing than we had intended, for when we found a droshky the driver wanted our fare before we got on. But I let loose with a volley of Polish curses and threatened that if he did not let us get into his droshky at once, we would yank him off the driver's seat. This worked; without another word, the driver let us climb aboard and took us to Dr. Alexander's place.

On the way, I could hear gunfire from the direction of the ghetto. My heart ached for my father and for Pela's parents. I wanted to get back to Zambrzyniec but I realized that I could not abandon Max. I would have to stay with him until I was sure that he was safe.

Dr. Alexander carefully examined Max's arm. Then he looked straight at Max and gave his diagnosis. "If you want to keep that arm, young man, you'd better have that bullet removed. I can't do that here in my office. You'll have to go to a hospital."

I took Max back to Maria's apartment and told her what the doctor had said. There was no question in my mind but that Max would lose his arm, if not his life, unless the bullet was removed as soon as possible. But what would he gain if a doctor or nurse at the hospital would become suspicious and report him to the Germans? Maria suggested a small Catholic hospital in her neighborhood. She said that the nuns there did not ask too many questions. She did not know how the nuns felt about Jews, but she had heard that they had already treated many wounded members of the Polish underground. If we were to tell them that Max was an underground fighter, they probably would not be too inquisitive.

So Maria and I took Max to the hospital. While I sat him down on the steps which led to the entrance, Maria went inside and informed the house doctor that one of her friends, a member of the Polish underground, had just been wounded in the arm and was in need of immediate surgery. The doctor agreed to admit Max. After the operation, Max remained in the hospital for twelve days. Then—as I was to learn only years later—the doctor told him that he had better leave because there was talk among the other patients in his ward that he was Jewish. If these rumors came to the ears of the Gestapo, the doctor said, he and the whole hospital would be in trouble for treating a Jew.

Max therefore went back to Maria's apartment. Somehow, Maria Krupka found out that Max's brother Jozef was still inside the ghetto. She sent a message to Jozef by an underground courier that since Max was hurt and she could no longer keep him at her sister's apartment, it would be best for Max to return to the ghetto, where Jozef could care for him until some opportune moment when both young men would be able to escape into the "Aryan sector." Max returned to the ghetto. He was among those killed in the Warsaw ghetto uprising in April, 1943.

But I am getting ahead of my story.

After settling Max safely—as I thought—in the hospital, I set out for the railroad station to catch the train for Lochow. As I walked down Mlynarska Street, I was held up by two husky young Poles. They turned up the lapels of their jackets, showing me a badge that did not look familiar but quite official. "We're from the police," one of them said. "Show us your papers." I had heard of such incidents before. Many Poles were making a lucrative business out of "fishing" for Jews in the "Aryan sector" of Warsaw. When they saw someone whom they suspected of being a Jew, they would display an official-looking badge and demand all his money, threatening him that if he did not pay them off, they would report him to the Gestapo. Sometimes, they would continue tailing him until they found his hideout. Once they knew their victim's address they would turn up wherever he went, holding him up for more cash or scarce goods. When they saw that there was nothing more to be squeezed out of him, they would report him to the Gestapo and receive a cash reward for their cooperation with Hitler's New Order.

But the two young men on Mlynarska Street had the wrong person. Instead of answering them, I only laughed and heaped Polish curses upon them. This apparently left them at a loss for a reply. Just then a streetcar passed. I gave one of the hoodlums a swift kick and, before his partner had a chance to react, I had jumped onto the streetcar's open rear platform and was moving rapidly toward the center of the car. "Two SS men were following me," I panted to the other passengers. If there was anything the Poles hated thoroughly, it was the SS. Since I looked so completely Polish, I hoped that the other passengers would not think that the Germans had been following me because I was a Jewish fugitive. Luck was with me once again. The passengers rose from their seats, gathered around me and drew me into a tight circle to hide me from view, nodding their heads in delight at having saved one of their countrymen from the Germans.

Late in the evening, I arrived in Zambrzyniec, where Pela and Jasia were waiting for me.

Now came the ordeal of telling Pela that her parents and my father had probably gone to Treblinka. This time Pela's fortitude deserted her. She collapsed. She berated herself for having agreed to leave the ghetto without her parents. For several days I feared that she would lose her mind. But one morning she got out of bed and assured me that she had no intention of letting go. She knew that she would have to keep her sanity, she said, if not for my sake, then certainly for the sake of our child. Pela and I were both determined to keep Jasia alive, even if it would take our last breath. Only if something were to happen to

Jasia would Pela and I cease to care whether we lived or died.

12

That August of 1942, Pela and I started a new life, a life of constant posing and pretending to be what we were not, in order that our child and we might live. We had to forget our Jewish names and memorize the names and dates on our new "Aryan" papers so perfectly that, no matter what happened, we would not give ourselves away. During the night, we would wake each other and "rehearse" our new biographical details to make certain that even in our sleep we would not say anything to reveal our true identity.

One morning I borrowed a bicycle from one of the Slovik boys and pedaled to Lochow. There, at the general store, I bought two gold crosses on thin gold chains, one for Pela and one for Jasia. I also bought a Catholic prayer book for Pela, and some pictures of saints to hang on the walls of our room at Mrs. Slovik's farmstead. We kept the prayer book prominently displayed on our table so that whoever entered the room would see it at once. Every evening, before bedtime, Pela knelt with Jasia before the pictures of the saints and recited prayers from her Catholic prayer book, often leaving the door of our room open so Mrs. Slovik would be able to hear her praying.

During our first two weeks in Zambrzyniec I made several trips to Warsaw. As far as Mrs. Slovik and her neighbors knew, I was traveling on business for the lumberyard at which I was supposed to be employed. But the true reason for my visits to Warsaw was to obtain a *Kennkarte* (identity card) and an *Arbeitskarte* (a certificate of employment carried by Polish non-Jews). Every Pole who was employed had such a card, and I felt that if for some reason I would ever run into trouble with the police, this card could save my life. In the middle of August, 1942, I received forged *Arbeitskarten* for Pela and myself, certifying that we were both employed at a lumberyard near Lochow.

On these trips to Warsaw I usually had to remain in the "Aryan sector" overnight. I would stay with Frank Piasecki, my father's "friend" from Poznan, whom my father had helped so much but who in return had permitted my stock of ladies' hose to vanish from his store. I had no other choice of lodging because the apartment of the "underground artist" on Jerozolimska Avenue was not available. As for Piasecki, I knew he was not an honest man, but I also felt instinctively that he was not the type of Pole who would go out of his way for anything, including opportunities to harm Jews; neither would his wife, who was a devout Catholic. Piasecki had only one fear: he did not want to be caught hiding Jews in his apartment. Bulletins had been posted throughout German-occupied Poland warning all Poles that anyone caught giving aid or shelter to Jews would be subject to the death penalty. I must therefore give full credit to Mr. Piasecki for agreeing to have me spend a night now and then at his apartment, as long as he did not have to put up an extra bed for me. I slept in his kitchen, on the floor.

As I left Mr. Piasecki's apartment after one of these overnight visits I met in front of his house a woman named Christina, whom I remembered from the days before the war. She had been a maid at the home of a Jewish family I had known. Now she told me that she had with her a baby girl, one year old, a granddaughter of the people for whom she had been working. She had smuggled the child out of the ghetto in order to save it,

133

and she had acted just in time, too, for shortly thereafter, the child's parents and grandparents had been killed by the Germans. An unmarried woman in her thirties, Christina passed the little girl off as her own illegitimate baby and had had her baptized at the parish church. She could not take another job because she had to care for the child. She had heard that Pela and I had escaped from the ghetto. What was I doing back in Warsaw? she wanted to know. And where were Pela and my baby? When I told Christina that we were living as "Aryans" in the countryside, she said that she was very lonely and would be happy to move into the country in order to be near us. Also, she said, she might be able to protect us in case the Germans were after us. Touched by Christina's offer, I told her to hurry home, pack her things and come back to Zambrzyniec with me.

I introduced Christina to our landlady, Mrs. Slovik, as a cousin whom we had invited, along with her baby daughter, to spend her vacation with us. The baby—she had been baptized Marysia—had dark hair and a dark complexion, but it did not occur to anyone that she might not be Christina's child, because Christina, too, was dark-haired. In fact, unlike Pela, Jasia and myself, who could pass for typical Poles, Christina, a one hundred per cent devout Catholic of impeccable Polish ancestry, looked quite Jewish. Nevertheless, she had nothing to fear from the Germans because she had all her papers and was able to trace back her "Aryan" descent even beyond the obligatory two sets of "Aryan" grandparents. Christina proceeded to teach Pela all the Polish Catholic customs and took her to church with her every Sunday. If Pela became known as a regular worshipper at the parish church, Christina said, we would quickly make friends and be safe from suspicion. I, however, was afraid to go to church because I feared that I would feel awkward there and that some word or gesture on my part might give me away. So I did not accompany Pela and Christina to mass but remained at home, arguing that someone had to stay with the two little girls, Jasia and Marysia.

Before we knew it, the summer was gone, and the vacationers went back to the cities. Pela and I had to think up some explanation for Mrs. Slovik why we wanted to stay on in Zambrzyniec. I hit upon a happy idea. One afternoon I announced to Pela joyously and just loud enough for Mrs. Slovik to hear that the lumber firm with which I was employed had transferred me to the Zambrzyniec area to measure trees in the surrounding woods. (I did not know how one measured trees, but I had learned from the Galewski brothers that trees were measured before they were cut down for lumber.) For our landlady's benefit, Pela and I even staged a loud argument, with Pela protesting that she did not want to spend the fall and winter in this one-horse town but finally giving in because my firm insisted on my transfer so that we had no choice in the matter.

The truth, of course, was that I had no job and that our funds were running low. Christina proved to be a blessing, for she offered to share her own meager savings with us.

But we had hardly established our "credentials" in Zambrzyniec when a minor crisis threatened to upset everything. Late in September I developed a boil. At first I paid no attention to it, but then the trouble spread until my whole body, except for my face, was covered with boils. I was unable to sit or to lie on my back or stomach. When one boil burst and disappeared, it was replaced almost immediately by a crop of new pus-filled swellings. I knew I had to get medical help but to whom was I to turn? I could not go to a doctor in Zambrzyniec or in the

135

surrounding area because even a routine physical examination would give me away at once. In Poland at the time only Jewish males were circumcised.

I decided that, miserable though I was with pain, and risky though it would be, I would have to go to Warsaw once again and see Dr. Alexander, who had attended to my friend Max and who was known to be kind to underground fighters, even those whom he suspected of being Jewish.

Dr. Alexander said that my boils had come from malnutrition. He gave me an injection and advised me to eat as many onions and carrots as I could. He probably thought that these two common vegetables would be the ones most accessible even to a member of the underground who was on the move all the time.

I followed Dr. Alexander's advice with regard to carrots, but I avoided onions because I did not want to attract attention to myself in any way, and I thought that if anything would destroy my cherished anonymity it would be an oniony breath.

My fight against the boils took over three months. I think they were caused not only by malnutrition but also by the mental and emotional stress I was undergoing and the unsanitary conditions under which we were living on Mrs. Slovik's farm.

While I was still slowly recovering, Pela and I narrowly escaped being caught. We wanted to go to the market, which was about three or four miles from Zambrzyniec, to buy two straw pallets for Jasia and Marysia. Christina, who had found lodging on a farm near Mrs. Slovik's, came to our room with Marysia to stay with Jasia while Pela and I were away. Marysia was not well; she was sick with what later turned out to be dysentery.

Pela and I left Mrs. Slovik's farm very early that morning. It was a bright, sunny day. When we arrived at the

136

market place we noticed people scurrying back and forth. They seemed frightened and confused. Then we saw several German army trucks. We realized that the market place was surrounded by German troops. German soldiers were mingling with the crowds of shoppers. This was a "manhunt" such as the Germans periodically conducted to recruit Polish manpower for work. In such a "manhunt" the Germans would close in on a place of public assembly, round up as many Poles as possible and take them to a central assembly point where they were given a physical examination. Those who passed the examination were assigned to work on farms or were sent to labor camps in Germany. Those who were too old or too weak for heavy work were usually released and allowed to return to their homes.

Pela and I knew that if we were caught now, our fate was sealed. The physical examination would immediately show me up as a Jew and that would be the end. But we tried to remain calm. I remembered the *Arbeitskarten* which I had acquired for Pela and myself in Warsaw in order to "legitimize" us as true Poles if ever the need arose. Perhaps if we could prove that we were working at a lumberyard the Germans would consider us "essential" to the war effort and leave us alone. So we pulled our *Arbeitskarten* from our pockets and held them clutched tightly in our hands. A German soldier was moving toward us. He carried a rifle topped by a bayonet. Another German soldier was standing nearby and it seemed to me that he was looking straight at Pela and me. I decided to act before either of the two Germans made the first move. We marched straight up to the soldier with the bayonet, showed him our *Arbeitskarten* and explained to him that the other soldier had just let us go because we were engaged in "essential" work. The soldier seemed to believe us, but he tried to catch the eye of his partner.

This was our chance to escape. Drawing Pela along with me, I took several steps backward, then turned and very slowly, casually, walked away, holding Pela tightly by the hand. Once we had passed the German army trucks that surrounded the market place we broke into a run and made for a cornfield nearby. The corn had already been harvested and the stubble was sharp but we took off our shoes and raced across the field without looking back even once. Only after we had already covered a considerable distance did we stop for a moment and look back at the market place. We could still see the crowds and the trucks, and then we heard gunfire. We ran on. Finally, exhausted, we returned to Zambrzyniec. We proudly told every Pole we met the story of how we had eluded the German "manhunt." "We Polacks aren't as stupid as the Germans seem to believe," I said. The purpose of all this big talk, of course, was to present myself to the villagers as a true Polish patriot. If Pela and I not only looked like pure-bred Poles but also acted the part, I believed, no one in the village could possibly suspect that we were Jews.

Our friend Christina, however, was very much upset. She had news for us. While we had been away, two Polish policemen, accompanied by a German, had come to the Slovik farmstead. They had told Christina about rumors to the effect that she and her little girl were Jewish. Christina had emitted a stream of Polish curses, telling off the Polish policemen for being stupid enough to suspect anyone on the Slovik farm of being a dirty Yid. To see whether Christina was telling the truth, the German, who spoke no Polish, ordered the two Poles to question Christina about Polish Catholic rituals and customs of which Jews were not likely to be aware. Being a truly devout Catholic, Christina knew much more about her religion than her interrogators. She held forth to them at some length about intricate questions of Catholic faith and observance until the three men were exhausted and eager to get away from her. As they walked to the door, they mentioned quite casually that, according to information they had received, a young family from out-of-town had been staying at the Slovik farm. Where were they? Christina said that Pela and I were away and would not be back for another few days. Thereupon the two Poles and the German left, but warned that they would pursue the matter further.

Pela and I did not know what to do. Should we leave the village? Most probably everyone in Zambrzyniec had seen the policemen and had guessed at the purpose of their visit. Although the Polish peasants in Zambrzyniec and the surrounding villages hated the Germans, they were ready to collaborate with them when it came to handling Jews. We knew that if they found Jews hiding out in the area, they had no scruples about reporting them to the Gestapo, particularly since the Germans generously rewarded such collaboration. For every Jew reported to the Gestapo the reward was one kilo of sugar and the clothes stripped from the victim at the time of his arrest.

If we ran away from the village, I reasoned, the peasants might become suspicious, pursue us and report us to the Gestapo. After some discussion, Pela, Christina and I decided that our best defense would be to remain where we were, in the hope that the rumors would spend themselves and the police would not return. Pela and I planned to make ourselves very visible in the village streets and to stop villagers for small talk whenever possible so that we should be considered part of the village community.

We spent the next few days in a state of great anxiety. We slept very little and were constantly on the lookout for the police. It turned out that we had done the right thing in not running away, for the police did not return. Probably the police had made inquiries among the villagers, and the villagers told them that we must be proper Poles because if we had been Jews we certainly would have gone into hiding after the visit from the police. Instead, Pela and I were seen all over the village, socializing with the villagers, and we would hardly be doing that if we were Jews afraid of being caught.

About a week after our adventure at the market place little Marysia's condition grew worse. She could keep no food and quickly shriveled to skin and bones. Since the doctors in the village could do nothing for Marysia, Christina decided to return to Warsaw and take the child to a hospital there. She left us with a heavy heart because she really loved us and was concerned about our future, but she said she had no other choice if Marysia was to stay alive. A few days later we received a postcard from Christina in Warsaw. "Marysia died today. Pray for her soul." This was the last we ever heard of Christina. We never saw her again.

13

About two weeks after Christina's departure I found a job in a lumberyard. This lumberyard was just outside the town of Sadowne, about 40 miles from Zambrzyniec, near Malkinia, the railroad junction where Jews began the final lap of their journey to Treblinka.

I came to the lumberyard in search of a job as a clerk or bookkeeper. The manager told me that no help was needed in the office. But I was badly in need of work, not only because our money was running out but also for the purpose of making myself "credible" as an "Aryan." So I said to the manager that I would gladly start as an ordinary laborer. He looked at me with some suspicion. Why, he wanted to know, would a man of my aristocratic appearance and educational background want to become a plain laborer in a lumberyard? I explained to him that I had been an officer in the Polish army. Under German law, all former Polish officers had to register with the occupation authorities. But as a true Polish patriot (I hinted that I had important connections in the Polish underground) I did not want to degrade myself by registering with the Germans. For this reason I had left Warsaw and was willing to work at any job as long as it afforded me an adequate living. My argument convinced the manager, and I was hired.

Since the distance between Zambrzyniec and Sadowne made it impossible for me to commute between the two places every day, we had to leave Zambrzyniec and move to Sadowne. We wanted to make the move as inconspicuously as possible. We hired a horse and wagon from a peasant who lived in a town some distance away and left the village late at night.

In Sadowne I rented one room for the three of us in a tiny cottage perhaps 100 yards from the railroad tracks. The cottage belonged to Jozef Rukat, an unemployed railroad worker. Jozef lived in the cottage with his wife and their two children, a son, Marian, who was about 18 years old, and a younger daughter, Lily. The family was slovenly, lazy and illiterate. The cottage had only two small rooms, each perhaps ten feet square, but the Rukats were forced to take tenants because Jozef had been out of work for months and the money was badly needed.

Compared to our new accommodations, our room on the Slovik farmstead in Zambrzyniec had been a palace. The Rukat cottage was a dilapidated, flimsy frame dwelling, the kind which, before the war, would be rented out only to summer vacationers. Under normal conditions no one would have considered living there at any other time of year. The boards of the wooden floors were so badly warped and shriveled with age and weather that there were spaces between the boards wide enough for us to see the ground underneath. There was a constant draft from the floor. Our room, like that into which the four Rukats were crowded, had one wood-burning stove with a narrow pipe that pierced the wall. It was now October and I did not anticipate the winter season in this dwelling with any great joy.

The Rukat cottage was about a mile and a half from the lumberyard. Before the war, this lumberyard had belonged to a wealthy Polish family by the name of Radzio. The Germans had expropriated the lumberyard but had retained one of Radzio's sons, Karol, a man about my age, as manager. This was the man who had hired me. Radzio's family lived in Lochow, while he himself lived in a cottage on the grounds of the lumberyard, where his needs were attended to by a housekeeper named Wanda.

In addition to Karol Radzio, several other executives lived on the grounds of the lumberyard. Perhaps the most important of these executives was an SS officer named Astmuss, who had been assigned by the German authorities to supervise this lumberyard and several other lumberyards in the area. This position was regarded as a prize job because it kept Astmuss out of active service in the German army. At first I did not know that Astmuss was an SS man because he never wore his uniform on the job. A man in his early forties, he was married and had two or three children, but like Radzio's family, they, too, did not live with him. They had remained in Danzig, where Astmuss had been born and raised. Like Radzio,

Astmuss, too, employed a housekeeper. She was a young Polish woman in her late twenties, whose name was Felicia. It was no secret that Felicia was her employer's mistress and an avowed Nazi collaborator who hated both Poles and Jews.

The chief bookkeeper of the lumberyard, who also lived on the grounds, was Adolf Lieberbauer, a good-looking man in his forties. His family life was above reproach. His wife, Janina, and their son, Paul, a boy of about five, were living with him. I was told that Lieberbauer was a *Volksdeutscher*, a Polish citizen of German descent. He was Astmuss' right hand and apparently enjoyed the complete confidence of the SS man, for whenever Astmuss was away on official business, which happened often, Lieberbauer was left in charge.

A cottage next to the Lieberbauers was occupied by two families, the Nowakowskis, who owned the cottage, and a childless couple, Edward and Marta Mamia. The Nowakowskis, a family of five, lived in two rooms on the first floor. Mr. Nowakowski, a man in his fifties, had been working as a clerk for the Radzios before the war. Now their son, a young man of about 20, was employed as a yard supervisor in the lumberyard. Also living at home with their parents were two daughters—Sophie, a very pretty girl of 18, and Helen, who was 14. The Nowakowskis were a very conservative family, staunch Catholics who hated the Germans. They seemed to be decent people. They led a quiet, withdrawn life, hoping that by minding their own business they would be able to keep out of trouble until Poland was free again.

The Mamias, two middle-aged people, occupied the second floor. They had lived in Poznan before the war. Like Frank Piasecki, they had been expelled from Poznan by the Germans in order to make room for citizens of the *Reich*. Edward and Marta were a happy-go-lucky pair, always laughing and joking, and ready to make friends with everyone in the lumberyard. Before the war Poznan had been known as a hotbed of anti-Semitism, but as far as we could judge, Edward and Marta, like the Nowakowskis, would not go out of their way to make trouble for Jews.

Directly behind the Nowakowski home lived Edward Mamia's brother, Roman, with his wife. Like Edward, Roman had been expelled from Poznan and had obtained a supervisory job at the lumberyard. He had a slight limp because one of his legs was shorter than the other. Roman and his wife, Barbara, were the opposite of Edward and Marta. They were very quiet, reserved people who rarely laughed and seemed to think it was a sin to enjoy life.

Except for Radzio and Astmuss, these executives did not earn a high salary. So they used other devices to help make ends meet. If a peasant came to the lumberyard with his wagon to pick up an order of lumber, they would throw in a few additional boards for which the peasant would pay them directly in the form of chickens, eggs, milk, sour cream or butter. These foods were at a premium because they were strictly rationed; most meat and dairy products had been requisitioned for the Germans. They could be obtained without ration cards on the black market, but only at exorbitant prices which the average Pole could not afford. The lumberyard executives therefore considered themselves fortunate to have such reliable suppliers of food, and it seemed that Radzio and Astmuss turned a blind eye to this petty embezzlement.

Pela and I made a point of getting to know my fellow workers as quickly as possible. We felt that if we cultivated their friendship and won their trust, it would not occur to them to wonder where we had come from or to suspect us of being anything but Poles. We made friends

144

with several such families, who lived not far from the lumberyard.

There was Mr. Kujawa, a man in his late fifties, who was working in the boiler room. He and his wife lived in a one-room hut in back of the lumberyard. They shared this room, plus an attic, with what seemed to us like at least a dozen children ranging in age from about three to seventeen. The children were always barefoot, wore clothing that was obviously home-made, and were indescribably filthy. So were their parents, neither of whom was able to read or write.

A hut adjoining that of the Kujawa family was the home of the Zielinskis, who were a better type. The father, Stanislaw, was the chief mechanic at the lumberyard. He was something of a crackerbarrel philosopher who enjoyed talking politics and made no secret of his contempt for Hitler and the Germans. The Zielinskis had only two or three children. Unlike Kujawa's wife, Mrs. Zielinski was a meticulous housekeeper, and the two rooms in which the Zielinskis lived were always spotless.

There was one worker to whom I took a particular liking almost from the start. He was Walus Radziejewski, a boy of 17 who was employed as a timekeeper. He was altogether different from any of the other men I met in the lumberyard. Blond and blue-eyed, he was an exceptionally handsome young man. Also, he was softspoken and courteous. I could tell that he came from a cultured, educated home. He did not live on the premises but at home with his parents in a village about a mile from the lumberyard.

In addition to the people I have mentioned, the lumberyard employed some 50 unskilled laborers who sawed the wood, and loaded, unloaded and stacked the lumber. Most of them lived in neighboring villages. The town of Sadowne itself, about three miles away, was linked to the lumberyard by a highway, bordered on each side by large, dense woods.

On the other side of the railroad tracks near the lumberyard were two individuals whom I mistrusted and feared from the very beginning because they were both vociferous Jew-baiters. The one was Baran, a young man of 30, who was in charge of what was known as the "produce warehouse." Located near the railroad tracks, this was the place to which the peasants from the surrounding countryside were required to bring part of their crops and produce for shipment to Germany. Baran lived in a cottage with his younger sister. Part of his cottage was occupied by the stationmaster of the Sadowne railroad depot, a man named Romanowski, and his family. The home of the Romanowskis looked like a church. It was filled with religious paintings and sculptures. In front of their cottage stood a beautiful statue of Mary and the infant Jesus. I often saw Romanowski kneeling in front of this statue with his eyes closed, apparently immersed in his prayers. However, I found out that this was not a godly individual. He was a Nazi collaborator who had many Jewish lives on his conscience.

This was the setting in which I lived and worked for fourteen months—from October, 1942 until late in December, 1943.

I reported for work each morning at 7 o'clock. Most of the time I worked the regular shift of eight hours, but sometimes I was lucky and got an opportunity to work overtime, with overtime pay. My job involved heavy physical labor. I loaded and unloaded lumber from railroad cars and stacked it in the yard. Every night I brought home with me a big sack of lumber remnants to use as firewood for our stove. Soon after supper, the fire would go out and our room became bitter cold, with icy drafts blowing in through the decaying walls and floor. I

146

would get up each morning at 4 o'clock to rekindle the fire in our stove so that the room would be warm by the time Pela got up to prepare breakfast for Jasia.

That fall Jasia became ill with the same symptoms as Christina's little Marysia. She was unable to retain any food and was racked day and night with cramps and diarrhea. Pela and I were terrified that she might die just as Marysia had. So Pela finally took Jasia on the 80-mile journey to Warsaw to see what could be done for her in the city. She was afraid to seek help at a hospital, where she might be asked too many questions. But she learned that Dr. Stankiewicz, a Pole whom she had known before the war as one of Warsaw's outstanding pediatricians, was still practicing in the city. Dr. Stankiewicz told Pela that he would get Jasia admitted to a children's hospital, but Pela declined his offer, explaining that we had no money to pay the hospital bills. The doctor shrugged his shoulders and handed her a box of pills. Pela would never have dared leave our baby in a hospital, especially not since we lived so far away from the city. So she brought Jasia back home and we prayed that with the help of Dr. Stankiewicz's pills and our own loving care our child would survive and recover.

It took three weeks before we could give Jasia halfway normal food, but her strong constitution won out and she recovered. Still, she was very pale and thin and Pela and I wondered how she would survive the winter in our cold, drafty room. It was only November, but temperatures were already below freezing.

Pela did everything she could to get us accepted as trusted members of the lumberyard community and to forestall the possibility of anyone starting a rumor, as had happened in Zambrzyniec, that we were Jews. Every Sunday she joined our landlady, Mrs. Rukat, for the five-mile walk to church. At first Pela felt uneasy about praying in a church but she told herself that as long as she believed in God, it did not make any difference how one worshipped Him, especially not when it was a question of life and death. She felt that what she was now asking from God was really not so very much: Let Jasia survive, and, if possible, let us, her parents, survive as well. I still could not bring myself to go to church with Pela. Coming from a less devoutly Jewish background than Pela, I had no qualms about participating in a church service, but I was still afraid, as I had been in Zambrzyniec, that something I might say or do during the service might give both of us away.

In addition to going to church with our landlady, Pela made a point of spending as much time as possible with her. She often hinted to Mrs. Rukat that we were in the Polish underground and that this was why we were leading such a withdrawn life, away from the city and its distractions. Together with several other women from Sadowne, Mrs. Rukat and Pela engaged in a little business enterprise. About three times each week they would go to the produce market of Sadowne to buy butter, cheese and chickens from the peasants there. They would then take these purchases by train to Warsaw, where they would sell them at outdoor market places for a small profit. Mostly this "profit" would amount to little more than a few zlotys and perhaps some butter or sour cream, but Pela was satisfied.

Usually, on these trips to Warsaw, which took two and one-half hours each way, Pela would take Jasia with her, not only because I had to go to work and she did not want to leave the child with strangers, but also because she had been told that as a rule Poles accompanied by small children would not be picked up by the Germans during the "manhunts" which by then had become frequent occurrences also in Warsaw. But the trips to Warsaw were hard on Jasia, who was not yet two years old. I would have to wake Pela and Jasia at three o'clock in the morning. Pela would wrap a shawl around herself and Jasia and carry Jasia in her arms to the Sadowne depot, which was a mile and a half from our place. Most of the winter Pela had to walk through deep snowdrifts to get to the depot. It was lucky that Jasia was a remarkably good and placid child. When we took her from her warm crib and bundled her up in warm wraps for the trip, she hardly opened her eyes and did not make a sound. Sometimes it almost seemed to us she knew that her mother was making these trips to Warsaw for her sake, so that she should have enough good food to pull her through the winter.

In Warsaw, we had made contact with a man whom we had known before the war and who was to prove a much better friend to us than Frank Piasecki. He was Stomatos Kokkinakis, a Greek businessman in his sixties. Kokkinakis owned a halvah factory. Before the war, one of my uncles had worked for him as chief bookkeeper; Pela, too, had been employed there briefly as an office clerk. Mr. Kokkinakis had valuable business connections. There were in Poland some Italians who had been in the same business as he. Since Italy was now an ally of Nazi Germany, the Italians in Poland were accorded almost the same privileges as the Germans and were in a position to obtain foods which had all but vanished from Polish homes. We remembered Mr. Kokkinakis as a splendid person, and during the early months of the war we heard stories of how he had helped Jews with food, money and good advice. The story went that he had been summoned by the Gestapo several times for interrogation, but somehow had managed to keep out of prison.

Now it occurred to Pela that she should seek him out again. Perhaps he would be able to get candy or fruit for

Jasia. So, on one of her early trips from Sadowne to Warsaw, Pela, carrying Jasia in her arms, rang the bell of Mr. Kokkinakis' house. Her heart hammered as she waited for the door to open. She did not know what kind of reception she would get. But she need not have worried. Mr. Kokkinakis and his maid, Anna, welcomed her warmly and invited Pela and Jasia to stay for dinner. During the meal, Anna went out and bought Jasia a pretty little cross on a chain and took it to her church to be blessed before placing the chain around Jasia's neck. Mr. Kokkinakis gave Pela several pounds of candy to sell in Sadowne.

Before long Jasia came to look forward to these visits. She grew to love the old gentleman who took her on his lap and played with her as her grandfathers might have, had they been alive.

Although I encouraged Pela to make the trips to Warsaw for Jasia's sake, I was very uneasy each time until they returned. It was forbidden for individuals who were not peasants to take food from the country to the city for sale; it was regarded as "smuggling." Frequently the police would turn up at train stations between Sadowne and Warsaw, board the trains and confiscate food products carried by women passsengers. Men, of course, never engaged in this trade because it was much too risky for them. If a woman said that she was not planning to sell the food but was only taking it to relatives or friends, the Germans believed her much more readily than they would a man giving the same explanation.

I made it a rule to meet Pela and Jasia at the railroad station every time they returned from Warsaw. One day Pela arrived in a state of near-hysteria. At first she was not able to tell me what had upset her so, but at home, in our room, she finally told me. As the train approached Sadowne, she had looked out the window and had seen a

Joanne (Jasia) with her rag doll, in Sadowne, on her second birthday, January 14, 1943

May 1946: Aboard the SS *Marine Perch*
On our way to the United States (Joanne is at the right)

crowd. When she looked more closely she saw a scene she was never to forget. A Gestapo man was holding a baby by its legs. Another Gestapo man stood nearby, his gun at the ready. The Gestapo man threw the baby into the air and the other Nazi opened fire. The baby dropped to the ground. The two Gestapo men then kicked the dead baby with their boots, guffawing with pleasure.

I quietly listened as Pela, amidst racking sobs, told me the story. I knew that this was not the first time such a thing had happened on the railroad line between Sadowne and Warsaw, for, as I have already mentioned, the route from Warsaw to Sadowne was used also by the boxcar trains that brought Jews to Treblinka. Many parents would throw their babies from the train windows in the hope that perhaps someone with a kind heart might find the child and care for it, so that the child might have a chance to survive even if its parents did not. How were they to know that their babies would fall into the hands of the Gestapo even without ever reaching Treblinka?

In bed that night, Pela and I wept for this baby and for all the other babies who had suffered the fate from which we were trying so hard to protect our little Jasia. I pressed our pillows to our mouths and covered our heads with our blankets so that the Rukats, in the next room, should not hear us and ask us the next morning whether anything was wrong.

We did not want Mrs. Rukat to hear us weep, but we wanted to be very sure that she heard us pray. As on Mrs. Slovik's farmstead in Zambrzyniec, so here, too, Pela got down on her knees at bedtime each night and recited prayers from the Catholic prayer book, loud enough for the Rukats to hear. We knew that everything depended on our ability to convince the Rukats that we were a devout Polish Catholic family.

The mainstay of our daily diet in Sadowne was potatoes. For breakfast, at 5:30 or 6 in the morning, we
would have plain boiled potatoes without any butter or
fat. When I came home for the midday meal, there
would be potato soup made by boiling potatoes in water
with a few bay leaves floating on top for flavor. We had
neither bones nor fat to add to the soup. Supper was
plain boiled potatoes again, flavored this time with a little horseradish. On Sundays Pela prepared a special
treat: potato pancakes, fried directly on the red-hot lid of
our stove because we had neither oil nor fat with which
to grease the bottom of a frying pan. Whatever butter,
cream or eggs were left over from Pela's business deals
were, of course, saved for Jasia. On very rare occasions,
we got an apple. In that case, we would peel the apple
and let Jasia eat the flesh while Pela and I ate the peels.
Pela and I would fight over those apple peels; I wanted
her to have them all while she wanted to leave them all to
me. Most of the time I won: Pela would eat the apple
peels.

14

Despite the hardships and the uncertainties of our life
in Sadowne, Pela and I knew that we had much to be
thankful for. We were free, we had a roof over our heads,
and we had enough food to keep us from starvation.
From time to time we were given forceful reminders that
many Jews in Poland were not as fortunate as we.

Late one afternoon in December, 1942 Pela heard a
faint knock on our door. It was a Jewish woman in tatters, begging for food. Pela did not ask her where she had
come from; perhaps she had managed to escape from
some ghetto into the woods, where Jewish fugitives hid

from the Germans during the day, emerging only after dark to beg friendly peasants for a little bread or milk. At that time men were working on the railroad tracks within sight of our window and Pela knew it would be disastrous not only for this poor woman but also for us if these men saw Pela giving food to a Jewess. Nevertheless, Pela took the chance. She gave her the potatoes she had been cooking for our supper, adding a few raw potatoes and our last piece of bread. The woman's eyes filled with tears. "May God bless you and may your family never have to go through the hell I've seen," she said. Then she turned and walked away. But for the grace of God, Pela could have been in her place.

Pela was still pale and shaken when someone opened the door of our room without knocking. It was Marian, the Rukats' son.

"Did you give anything to that goddamn Jewess?" he asked Pela. "You know, she had the nerve to knock on our door, too. They're still around, goddamn them. Even the cold winter can't finish them off."

Now we knew it. The Rukats hated the Jews no less than they hated the Germans. Later I found out that the poor Jewish woman had once been a neighbor of the Rukats. I wondered why, if he and his parents hated the Jews so much, Marian had not grabbed her and turned her in to the Gestapo. But then, knowing Marian, I suppose he felt it was too cold for him to bother going out, even if it meant receiving a reward from the Germans for bringing in a Jew.

Another evening, about a week later, a young Jewish girl knocked at the Rukats' door. She was wrapped in flimsy rags and was shivering with the cold. We could hear her conversation with the Rukats. We gathered that the girl and her parents had once been tenants of the

153

Rukats; they had lived in the room which we now occupied. After the Germans had come, the family had fled
from Sadowne. Among the belongings they had left behind was a *tallith*, a woolen prayer shawl that had belonged to the father. Now the girl wanted her father's
tallith; she needed it for a little protection from the cold.
"You mean that woolen shawl with the black stripes,
Miss?" we heard Lilly, the Rukats' daughter, ask. "Sorry,
it's too late. I made myself a dress out of it." A few minutes later, through our window, we saw the girl, bent
over against the whistling wind, stumble away through
the snow toward the railroad tracks.

Pela quickly reached under our bed, where we kept our
few clothes in a cardboard box, and pulled out a kerchief
and a worn sweater. With these, she rushed out of the
cottage and followed the girl. When she caught up with
her, she gave her the sweater and the kerchief. "For you,"
she said. "Take it and don't ask me any questions." Then
Pela quickly turned away from the girl and trudged
through the snow back to our cottage. She had taken a
big chance to help this girl. Luckily our windows faced
the railroad tracks, while those of the Rukats faced the
other way; so the Rukats could not have seen her.

It caused Pela and me terrible anguish that she should
have to think twice before helping a fellow Jew in need.
But we knew that no matter how we felt, we had to think
of our little Jasia. We could not permit ourselves to do
anything that might endanger her well-being.

There were times when we saw Jews in agony and
could do nothing to help them. One afternoon, still in
December, when Pela went to the well near our cottage
to fetch some water, she saw a young Jewish man, one
side of his face bruised and swollen, his hands tied
behind his back, being driven away in a wagon by a
neighboring peasant. What had happened was quite

154

clear. The peasant had caught a Jewish fugitive, had given him a good beating and was now going to turn him over to the Gestapo. To this day Pela is haunted by the look she saw in the eyes of this poor Jew. After filling our bucket with water from the well, she ran into our room, her fist in her mouth to stifle her sobs. A poor, innocent man was being dragged to his death and she had stood right there, not able to offer him even a drop of water.

As the winter of 1942 wore on I noticed that Walus Radziejewski, the young, handsome timekeeper, looked at me with particular sympathy and tried to ease my work load whenever he could. At first I thought he was doing this only because he was such a sensitive young man and could see that I was not accustomed to doing hard physical work. But it struck me that he had begun to treat me with unusual deference, as if I, an ordinary workman, was his superior, and not he mine, as he was then.

One day I decided to find out more about this quiet, softspoken boy. Although I had never gone to church before, I now asked Walus whether he would walk to mass with me the following Sunday. He agreed and we met that Sunday morning at the railroad depot. We took the highway that led from the lumberyard to the town of Sadowne. I looked at the woods on either side of the highway. Then, on sheer impulse, I said to Walus, "Tell me, Walus, if some Jewish partisans were to jump out from these woods and attack us here, what would we do? We don't even have a stick with which to defend ourselves."

Walus looked at me and replied, "I don't believe that these poor hungry Jews would attack anyone. They're glad if they are left alone. They wouldn't attack innocent civilians."

Hearing this, I took the plunge. I told him that my wife and I were Jews, that we were badly in need of friends whom we could trust with our secret, and that somehow I felt that he, Walus, could be such a friend.

Walus stopped in his tracks. I saw his eyes fill with tears. Then he threw his arms around me. "I'm Jewish, too," he said.

We never got to the church that Sunday morning. Instead, we walked along the highway for hours, while Walus told me the story of his life. His family had lived in Lodz before the war. His father, Daniel Radziejewski, had been a well-known, prosperous textile manufacturer. Walus was his parents' only child. Their wealth, their Polish surname and their assimilated way of life had given the family an easy entry into Polish society. When the Germans came to Lodz, the family fled to the Russian sector. From there, they planned to go to Yokohama, Japan, where they intended to take a boat to the United States. They had some money in an American bank. But when they arrived in Vilna, the Radziejewskis had an unpleasant surprise. They learned that all Jews entering the Russian sector from the German-occupied part of Poland had to register with the Soviet authorities. When the Radziejewskis registered, they were asked about their plans for the future. When they explained that they did not intend to settle in Vilna but wanted to go to Japan as soon as possible, they were told that Jews unwilling to settle down and work in the Russian sector would either be deported to Siberia or sent back to the German zone. The Radziejewskis were stunned. The very mention of Siberia struck terror in their hearts. But they had never even entertained the thought of settling in the Russian sector of Poland. Like most Poles—Jews and Gentiles alike—they simply did not trust the Russians. After some intense soul-searching, they decided that they had only

156

one choice: to return to the German sector. They would not go back to Lodz but would settle somewhere in the Polish countryside. They were certain that, far away from the big cities, their Polish surname and their ample supply of cash would protect them from being suspected as Jews. Somehow, the family had found a home near Sadowne. Like other Jews who had chosen to live as "Aryans" in the Polish countryside, the Radziejewskis made every effort to blend into their new environment. Like many other villagers, Walus' father began to produce corn whiskey at his home for sale. Walus applied for a job at the lumberyard and, despite his youth, had been given a semi-executive position. Everyone in the village, Walus said, liked the Radziejewskis and it seemed to him that no one ever regarded them as anything but pure-blooded Polish Christians.

Walus and I agreed that our two families should meet. We soon became close friends and felt about each other almost like members of one family. However, we were careful not to be seen too much in each other's company. We feared that if one of us were caught, and the Germans would know of our relationship, they might succeed, under torture, in having us inform on one another. I noticed that although Walus and his parents acted quite cheerful when there were Poles around, they acted very depressed when we were together alone. All their energy seemed to have drained from them and they were looking to me for moral support. I do not know why they believed so firmly in me, but they were apparently convinced that as long as I was there to bolster their morale, we would all survive.

The month of December, 1942 was drawing to a close and we marked our first Christmas as Polish Christians. We made a point of outdoing our landlords, the Rukats, in preparing for the holiday. Because our room was so

157

tiny, we bought only a small Christmas tree and, instead of setting it up on the floor, suspended it from the ceiling. Pela proudly displayed the Christmas tree decorations Mr. Kokkinakis had sent from Warsaw and she made a point of telling the Rukats that they were gifts from relatives of ours.

On Christmas Eve we joined the other villagers in singing the traditional Polish Christmas carols and I think we succeeded in convincing even those of our illiterate neighbors who were basically suspicious of newcomers that we were good Polish Christians.

Jasia was approaching her second birthday. She was still a little pale from her illness and hardly ever smiled. Pela and I were in constant fear that she might become sick again and we deprived ourselves of many things in order to be able to get milk and farina for her. To brighten her spirits, Pela gave her a doll for Christmas. Pela had made it herself from rags she had found near the cottage. It was Jasia's only toy and she loved it very much.

The Christmas season of 1942-43 in Poland was not one of peace and good will. One cold night early in January, 1943, several days before Jasia's birthday, Pela and I went through a soul-searing experience. The temperature that night was well below freezing and the ground was covered with a thick blanket of snow. Pela and I were already sound asleep when we were awakened by the rattle of a passing railroad train followed by bursts of machine-gun fire. We could hear the train grind to a halt. I went to the window but did not light our petroleum lamp, so I was able to see only too clearly what was going on outside. The train was so long that I could not see the last car. Except for a few sparse trees, the distance between our cottage and the railroad tracks—

about 100 yards—was spanned by flat terrain, now a white expanse of heavy snow.

The train was one of the boxcar trains that were carrying Jews by the thousands to Treblinka. We had seen such trains pass many times before, and our hearts had contracted as we watched them pass, but something unusual was happening to this train and its human cargo. I saw figures scrambling from the train and running off in every direction. The Germans were shooting at them. Some of the figures tumbled to the ground and remained there, quite still; others tried to hide by burying themselves in the deep snow. Apparently these Jews had broken the doors of the boxcars from the inside and had jumped out. I saw mothers throwing their small children from the cars into the snow. The Germans did not attempt to give chase; all they did was shoot at the fleeing figures. They probably thought that it was not worth the effort. Those Jews whom they would not be able to kill would fall wounded and would eventually freeze to death in the snow. As for those whom the German bullets might miss, the local peasants could be relied upon to turn them over to the Gestapo for the usual reward of a kilogram of sugar and the victim's clothes.

After a while the train whistle gave a long, mournful hoot and the train began to move again. After the last car of the train had vanished from view, we could see silhouettes crawling over the brilliantly white ground. Pela and I stood glued to our window, kneeling on the cold, drafty floor so that no one outside would be able to see us. If only we could run outside, gather up at least some of these dark forms, take them into our room and find shelter for them! But then we looked at Jasia asleep in her crib. Did we have the right to risk the life of our baby for the slim chance that we might be able to rescue one or two strangers who, with luck, might make it on their own? If we were caught and killed, it would help neither Jasia nor the wretched prisoners in the snow outside.

There was a knock on our door. Pela quickly ran back to our bed and covered herself. I padded to the door, pretending that I had just been awakened by the noise. I opened the door: there stood all four Rukats—father, mother, son and daughter. I opened my mouth to speak but the Rukats did not seem particularly interested in what I might have to say. They were too excited.

"Mr. Bludovski! Mrs. Bludovski!" they chorused. "Didn't you hear the commotion outside? Some Jews just escaped from a train and the Germans started to shoot at them! They must have hit quite a few. Just think—all those Jews lying on the ground, ready for the taking! It's a windfall! We can go out, pick them up and turn them over to the Gestapo. We'll take their clothes, clean out their pockets and on top of that we'll get a reward from the Germans for bringing them in. Come on! Everybody else in the village is going, too, so we'd better hurry! Otherwise there'll be no Jews left for us to catch."

My blood froze in my veins. As so many times before, I felt like strangling all the four Rukats with my bare hands. But then I looked at Pela and our baby, and I unclenched my fists. I was surprised at the calm and the presence of mind with which I answered our landlords.

"I'm afraid I'll have to pass this one up," I said. "I can't leave my wife tonight. She's in terrible pain. I think she's having one of her gall bladder attacks." The Rukats murmured a few words about being sorry that I'd have to miss this great chance for getting sugar and clothes. Then they rushed out. I do not know what they thought of my excuse for not joining them, but I think they had come to believe Pela's repeated hints that I was a behind-the-scenes leader in the Polish underground. The Rukats might have been willing to collaborate with the Germans

160

against the Jews, especially for a reward, but at the same time they hated the Germans and longed for the day when Poland would regain her independence. Hence, they had a healthy respect for the Polish underground— as distinct from the Jewish partisans—and everyone connected with it.

Minutes after the Rukats had left we could hear moans and screams outside as the wounded Jews were dragged through the snow to barns and stables. The chase went on all night long. Pela and I remained wide awake in our beds, and Pela, as usual, covered her head with her blanket so that the Rukats, when they returned, would not hear her sobs. I kept soaking rags in the cold water in our bucket and placing them over Pela's eyelids so they should not be red and swollen when she faced our landlords the next morning.

At 6 o'clock the next morning I went to work as usual. I trudged through the snow alongside the railroad tracks and saw no bodies there. But when I arrived at the gate of the lumberyard there was a crowd of workers bent over something on the ground. I moved closer. On the ground, between two stacks of lumber, lay a blond girl, perhaps 18 years old. She was bleeding and unconscious; obviously, she was one of the Jews who had escaped from the death train the night before. She wore a heavy winter coat and a pair of black riding boots. One of the young fellows from the lumberyard was trying to pull off the girl's boots, but this was impossible because they were frozen to her legs. He ran into the factory building and returned with a hatchet. He was about to bring the hatchet down on the girl's legs when Stanislaw Zielinski, the chief mechanic, appeared on the scene. Zielinski raised his arm and hit the hooligan in the jaw so that he toppled to the ground. Later, I learned that the girl had died and that the man had come back and managed to pry the boots from her legs when no one else was around.

I entered the main building of the lumberyard. As I passed through the boiler room I saw a young boy, perhaps 16 or 17 years old, warming his hands near the boiler. When I returned five minutes later, he was no longer there. The laborers of the lumberyard, aided by peasants from the vicinity, were still rounding up the survivors from the deportation train. They were herding the Jews into a barn not far from the Rukats cottage. There, they stripped them of their last possessions and locked them in. They left them in this barn for the rest of the day and through the night that followed. The next morning they took them to Gestapo headquarters in Sadowne. Later, the heroes in the battle against the Jews came home with their loot: clothing and sacks of sugar. Some of the sugar they kept; the rest they sold on the black market for good money.

How can I describe what Pela and I felt, or the feelings of our new friends, the Radziejewskis, at witnessing this brutality without being able to lift a finger in defense of our fellow Jews? I only prayed that we might survive the war and that, when the Germans were gone, I should be able to flush out at least some of the criminals who had done this horrible thing. The executives of the lumberyard—the Nowakowskis and the Mamia brothers — had seen everything and had expressed outrage that the Germans could be so heartless, but they, too, were unable to do anything and unwilling to risk their own necks by talking too much about the affair.

Pela and I had reached a point where we seriously contemplated ending our lives. But there was Jasia. We could not let her die! We had to give her at least a chance to live. And so, for her sake, we pulled ourselves together and acted, at least when others were around, as if we did not have a care in the world. But we found ourselves becoming superstitious. For instance, one day that January, Pela accidentally burned a hole in her dress while she was standing at our stove cooking some potatoes. Pela herself suffered no injury and the damage to her dress was insignificant, but this incident left us worried for days. It seemed to us that burning any part of a garment was a sign of bad luck. We lived in dread of another tragedy, and feared that this time we ourselves would be the victims. At the end of that month, for two days, it seemed to me that our superstition was not unfounded. I almost lost Pela.

15

On the last Saturday in January, 1943, Pela set out on one of her journeys to Warsaw in order to buy some food for Jasia. I left work at 3 P.M. that day as usual, took Pela to the station and put her on the Warsaw train. Pela was to remain in Warsaw overnight, sleeping on the Piaseckis' kitchen floor, and to arrive back in Sadowne at 6:30 Sunday evening. Since this was a weekend and I was off from work part of Saturday and all of Sunday, Pela left Jasia at home with me.

At the depot we heard rumors that the Germans were meeting all the trains as they pulled into Warsaw and were arresting passengers at random. This was the Germans' way of punishing the Poles for successful sabotage operations or assassinations perpetrated by the Polish underground. I felt that Pela should not travel as long as there was any danger of her being arrested, but she insisted on going because we needed food for Jasia. So, with a heavy heart, I put Pela on the train, then returned to our room in the Rukats cottage to sit with Jasia.

It struck me that all through Sunday the Rukats were acting rather strangely toward me, somehow as if they felt sorry for Jasia and me. I tried to put this out of my mind, but I spent most of that day urging the hands of the clock to move faster so that Pela would come home.

At about 6 o'clock on Sunday evening I bundled up Jasia in her winter wraps and went with her to the depot to meet Pela's train. I carried Jasia into the station-master's office, which was heated by a potbellied stove. The stationmaster seemed surprised to see us. "What are you doing here?" he asked.

"We're waiting for my wife. She's due on the 6:30 train from Warsaw," I replied.

The stationmaster's eyes grew wide with surprise. When, he wanted to know, had Pela left for Warsaw?
I told him that she had left on Saturday afternoon.

"You might as well get it straight from me," the stationmaster said. "Nobody who arrived in Warsaw on

that train, or on any other train either yesterday or today, will be coming home." He explained that on Friday morning the Polish underground had blown up a train with several high-ranking Nazi officials aboard. By way of reprisal, the Germans had stopped every train that had arrived in Warsaw during the 48 hours that followed. This time they were not merely making the usual random arrests but were seizing all the passengers aboard each train — men, women and children. Someone in town who had a radio had told the stationmaster that, according to the latest news report, all these passengers had been taken to one of Warsaw's main prisons, the Pawiak, and there some of them had already been executed while others would be sent to labor camps in Germany.

"Mr. Bludovski," the stationmaster concluded, "you might as well go home. You've probably seen the last of your wife for a long, long time."

I stood paralyzed with shock, holding Jasia tightly in my arms. She began to cry, almost as if she knew that something terrible had happened to her mother. I told the stationmaster that I did not believe him. "I'll wait here at the station for her even if it takes all night," I said.

The 6:30 train from Warsaw pulled into the depot on schedule. Hardly able to breathe, I watched the train slow down. As the cars crept by, I peered through the windows. The train never even stopped because there was not one single passenger aboard. After the locomotive had reached the far end of the platform, it picked up speed again and before I knew it the train was gone.

The next train from Warsaw came in at 8 o'clock. This time the train stopped. I paced the platform, watching for Pela. One elderly woman, carrying a milk can, stepped from the last car. That was all. The train whistle blew and the train moved on.

The next train was due at 9 o'clock. I decided that it was too late and too cold for Jasia to stay in the depot. So I carried her home and put her to bed. I asked the Rukats to look in on her from time to time. Then I rushed back to the depot to meet the 9 o'clock train.

The train chugged into the depot just as I arrived. But this train, too, only slowed down, then picked up speed again and was gone. There were no passengers aboard.

I felt as if I was living through a nightmare. What was I to do? How could I find out what had happened to Pela? I wanted to go to Warsaw and look for her. But what was I going to do with Jasia? I did not want to leave her with the Rukats, but I was afraid to take her with me to Warsaw. If I was arrested on the train, I did not want

165

to have her with me. Two more trains from Warsaw were due in Sadowne that night. I decided to wait for them. If Pela was aboard neither of them, I would go home to Jasia and wait until the morning to make further plans.

The 10:30 train brought three women passengers. No others. I stopped one of the women and asked her whether she had heard anything about what was going on in Warsaw. She told me that she and the two others had not come from Warsaw but had boarded the train only two stops before Sadowne. So they knew nothing.

By midnight, despite the intense cold, I was bathed in perspiration. The thought that Pela had been arrested was too much for me to take in. If she had been asked to show her papers, all would be lost. I knew that her "Aryan" documents were very poor forgeries: they might be good enough for spot checks in the countryside, but would they help if she were interrogated at Warsaw police headquarters in a mass arrest?

When the midnight train pulled in I shouted "Zosia! Zosia!" at the top of my voice. The door of the first car opened. Karol Radzio, the manager of the lumberyard, and one woman came out. I asked them whether, by any chance, they had seen my wife. They said no; they had only boarded the train at the previous stop, in Lochow. I kept on shouting "Zosia! Zosia!" Suddenly I saw a figure leap from the last car of the train and come running toward me. "Adam! Adam!" It was Pela. She was trembling with sobs as I took her into my arms. I was close to tears. I kept stroking her arms and shoulders to be sure I was not dreaming. Radzio and the stationmaster came over to us. They both agreed it was a miracle that Pela had not been arrested.

Pela and I quickly left the depot and went home to our child.

That night, in bed, Pela told me the story of her journey and of her lucky escape. The train in which she had traveled to Warsaw on Saturday had been packed with civilians, all Poles, mostly women, carrying milk cans, or baskets filled with eggs, poultry and produce to sell in Warsaw. When the train pulled into Praga, a suburb of Warsaw, there was a commotion on the platform outside. All the passengers in Pela's car crowded to the windows to see what was going on. The train ground to a stop. Outside, Gestapo men with machine guns at the ready were lined up on either side of the tracks. Other Gestapo men boarded the train. *"Aussteigen!* (Everyone out!)"* they shouted.

Pela was terrified.

Outside, SS men ordered all the passengers to line up in columns four abreast and prepare their papers for inspection. In the turmoil that ensued, many of the women in the front columns attempted to work their way backward, thinking that in this way they might be able to escape. But Pela was too shocked to move. She remained where she had been placed — in the second column from the front. One woman standing near her attempted to move backward. An SS man immediately pounced on her and pushed her back into line. As a result, Pela was jostled out of her place and found herself in the third column, face to face with another SS man.

"Der naechste! Der naechste! (Next! Next!)"* the SS men bellowed. Each passenger had to step forward to show his papers, then move to the right, where a column of army trucks was waiting. By the time Pela's turn came, she had recovered her composure. She walked up briskly to the SS man, with her papers in her hand. "If you please, Mr. Officer," she said in Polish, "I have a very sick baby at home. She needs a special medicine. I'm on my way to Warsaw especially to pick it up."

167

The officer looked her up and down, seemed to think for a moment and then, without even glancing at Pela's papers, said in German, "*Links, bitte!* (To your left, please!)" The officer had to tap Pela's arm and repeat his orders before Pela finally moved to the left, away from the waiting column of army trucks. She was free! She could hardly believe it.

She walked through the tunnel which led to the street. She was the only passenger from that train to be released. As she passed through the station exit, she quickened her steps. She was relieved and excited. When she was already in the street, some yards away from the station, she saw two men in civilian clothes moving toward the station. Her relief had made her talkative and slightly foolish. She stopped the two men and warned them not to enter the station because the Germans were arresting all the people inside. "So what the hell are you doing around here, girlie?" one of the men snarled at her in an uncultured Polish accent. Pela feared she had talked too much. She muttered something to the effect that she, too, had been arrested but that she had been released to go home to her sick baby. "Then go ahead," the man said, "and next time don't talk to strangers in the street." They probably were Germans or Polish plainclothesmen.

Without another word, Pela moved on. Although it was not yet six o'clock, the streets of Praga were deserted. Pela understood that there must be some trouble in Warsaw, but she did not know what. A streetcar bound for downtown Warsaw stopped in front of her, but Pela did not dare board it. She thought that if the Germans were stopping trains they might be stopping streetcars, too, in order to arrest the passengers. So she walked all the way to Frank Piasecki's home, about seven miles from the station. Whenever she saw a German army truck pass, she ducked into the nearest doorway.

After walking for several hours she arrived at the Piaseckis' apartment building and rang the Piaseckis' bell. Some minutes passed before Mrs. Piasecki opened the door. When she saw Pela, her face turned white. "You of all people! Of all the times for you to come to Warsaw—a Jewish woman!" she exclaimed. "Well, you can't stay here this time, I can tell you that! There's a manhunt going on. The Germans are raiding apartments. All I need is to be caught with a Jewish woman in my house; then we'll all be shot. You'll have to find another place."

By that time Pela was at the end of her strength. When she had left Sadowne, she explained to Mrs. Piasecki, she had had no idea that anything unusual had been going on in Warsaw. She had found that out only after her train had been stopped in Praga and she herself had narrowly escaped being arrested. Then she turned to leave. Since she had no place to spend the night and it was obviously dangerous for her to stay in Warsaw, she wanted to return to the station and take the next train back to Sadowne. But then she remembered that the last train for that day had already left. So she would have to spend the night in Warsaw, after all. She would have to hide in some bombed-out shell until the next morning.

But then apparently Mrs. Piasecki had a change of heart. "You might as well stay here, Mrs. Starkopf," she said with a sigh. "You can't very well sleep in the street. You can sleep in my kitchen, on the floor, as usual. I'll get you some blankets. But remember, you'll have to get out of here as early tomorrow morning as possible."

Under ordinary circumstances, Pela's pride would have kept her from accepting Mrs. Piasecki's reluctant invitation, but this time she had no sensible alternative. Later that evening, Frank Piasecki brought home the latest reports of the "manhunt" in Warsaw. He said that he and his wife would probably not leave home for the next day or two because they did not want to be picked up in the street by Germans.

Pela lay on the kitchen floor all that night, unable to sleep. How would she get back to Warsaw the next day if the "manhunt" continued? She did not want to risk being arrested again. But she was also afraid that if she failed to return to Sadowne on Sunday evening and I would hear the reports from Warsaw, I might try to come to Warsaw and look for her. And if I was arrested and assigned to a labor battalion, the physical examination would demonstrate my true identity at once and my destination would not be a prison or a labor camp but torture and death. Pela was therefore determined to attempt the return trip on Sunday no matter what befell.

At eight o'clock Sunday morning the phone rang in the Piasecki apartment. It was a friend of Mrs. Piasecki's. "She'll be unable to go to church with us this morning," Mrs. Piasecki told her husband with a knowing wink. "She has a headache." This, Pela learned, was a prearranged code between the Piaseckis and their friends. If either of these two couples heard reports of a "manhunt" on a Sunday they would give the other couple this disguised warning to remain at home.

After breakfast Pela told the Piaseckis that she was ready to leave. The Piaseckis warned her to be careful but did not make a serious attempt to keep her from leaving. So Pela bade the Piaseckis good-by and left. At first Pela thought of walking to the Praga railroad station — despite her own experience the previous afternoon, she felt it might be safer than riding in a streetcar — but then a streetcar stopped at the corner near the Piaseckis' apartment house and Pela got on. She felt that she might not have the strength to walk another seven miles in the bitter cold within less than 24 hours. However, despite

170

the cold weather, she stayed on the open rear platform of the streetcar so that she could jump off at once in case the Germans came. The only other passenger on this platform was a middle-aged man.

At one stop, an elderly woman, dressed in black, approached the streetcar's rear platform but did not attempt to board it. "Ladies and gentlemen," she said in Polish, in a voice that was low but quite clearly audible to Pela and the other passenger, "your next stop is Lapanka." *Lapanka* is the Polish word for "catching." The message which this Polish woman meant to convey through Pela and the man beside her to the passengers inside the streetcar was that the Germans were waiting at the next stop to arrest passengers. Pela and the man jumped off the streetcar and Pela wanted to speak to the woman in black, but the woman only said, "Please get away from me." She was probably a member of the Polish underground. As Pela crossed the street, she furtively looked back and saw that the woman was still standing at the streetcar stop, waiting to give her warning about "Lapanka" to the next streetcar.

Pela waited for a streetcar from the opposite direction to stop and discharge passengers. She wanted to question the passengers in order to see whether the woman in black had been right. But there was hardly anyone on that streetcar. A little boy of about ten got off. When Pela asked him whether he had seen anything unusual going on, he told her that the SS men were holding up all the streetcars at a certain stop, arresting the passengers and loading them into army trucks. "They just didn't catch me," he boasted. "I was too little and too fast for them."

Pela decided to take no more chances. She walked the rest of the way to the Praga station. Every few minutes she stopped passers-by coming from the direction in which she was headed, and asked them what the situation was in the next few blocks. Though she had covered part of the way by streetcar, the walk to Praga still took her six hours because whenever she saw SS men standing on street corners she ducked into the nearest courtyard and remained there until the men had gone.

When Pela finally reached Praga station it was too late for her to make the train that would arrive at Sadowne at 6:30. There was something else, too: the streets near the station were black with people. Also, there were German army trucks filled with prisoners. Pela heard the prisoners shouting out their own names and the addresses of relatives, hoping that some passer-by lucky enough to elude arrest would hear and notify the proper people. Others were throwing from the trucks little slips of paper with messages to friends and relatives, complete with addresses. Men and women in the street were picking up these slips from the ground and passed them on to young boys who were darting in and out of the crowd. The boys were couriers from the Polish underground, who could be relied upon to deliver the messages.

The hours passed and the "manhunt" still continued. The last train from Warsaw to Sadowne, Pela knew, would leave Praga at a little after 9:30 P.M. After that, there would be no more trains until the next morning. By that time, she thought, I might already be desperate enough to make the trip to Warsaw. She was so upset that she began to cry. An elderly Pole asked her, "Why are you crying? Is your husband on one of those army trucks?" Pela told him no, but that she had to get home to her sick baby in Sadowne, that the last train for Sadowne would be leaving soon, but that she was afraid to enter the station to buy her ticket because the Germans might arrest her.

"I have a suggestion," the man said. "I have a special pass. They can't arrest me. I can go into the station and

172

buy your ticket for you. You give me your money and then go into the ladies' room and wait for me. I'll knock on the door just before your train is ready to leave, so you'll be safe until it's time for you to get on the train." Pela had just enough money left to buy her return ticket. What if the man ran away with the money? But she felt that she had no alternative. So she gave him the 7 zlotys for the one-way ticket to Sadowne. Then she entered the station and with long strides headed straight for the ladies' room. Eventually, she heard a knock on the door. "Here's your ticket, missus," the man said. "Your train's just about ready."

Pela never had a chance to thank her rescuer, for after handing her the ticket, he vanished in the crowd. But after she had boarded the train she thanked God for having sent this man her way. At first she was not alone in the car; there was one old man, and an elderly woman with two milk cans. But after several stops, these people got off and Pela traveled the rest of the way to Sadowne alone.

The next day Pela was kept busy telling our neighbors of her adventures. They all agreed it was a sheer miracle that the SS man at Praga station had let her go. "Maybe you reminded him of his girl friend back in Germany," one of the neighbors volunteered with a sly grin.

16

In February, 1943, I received a promotion at the lumberyard: I was assigned to a supervisory job. As an "executive" I now had the option of living on the grounds of the lumberyard. We happily moved away from our room in Jozef Rukats' pigsty and rented a room in the cottage of the Nowakowskis, whose son was one of the yard supervisors. The five Nowakowskis—father, mother, son and two daughters — were quiet people who observed their religion and, as I have already said earlier, minded their own business. I did not know how they felt about Jews, but I intuitively sensed that they were basically honest people who, though they would not be likely to go out of their way to help Jews, probably would not take an active part in harming them.

Pela and I had no reason to believe that the Nowakowskis suspected us of being Jewish; like most of the other people in the lumberyard, they accepted our story that I had been an officer in the Polish army before the war. Along with many others in the lumberyard, the Nowakowskis also seemed to surmise that I had secret connections with the Polish underground, and this gave Pela and me added status among my fellow workers.

Our room at the Nowakowskis' was not much larger than the one we had occupied at the Rukats, but it was immaculate. Like the floors of many peasant homes in the Polish countryside, the floor of our new room was coated with red paint to keep it smooth and splinter-free. In the middle of the room there was the usual iron stove which served both for heating and for cooking. There was a double bed for Pela and myself, and a crib for Jasia. The walls were covered with pictures of Jesus, Mary, and a host of other saints popular among Polish Catholics.

Pela and I were determined that the Nowakowskis should never think of us as anything but good Polish Christians. So we started addressing postcards to ourselves, written in Polish, each in a different handwriting and signed by fictitious aunts, uncles and cousins. We would take these postcards with us on our trips to Warsaw, mail them from there to us in Sadowne, and then make sure that the Nowakowskis and the others in the lumberyard saw them. If you had many relatives who wrote to you regularly, it was hardly likely that you were Jewish. Jews in Poland in those days simply did not have families any more.

Nevertheless, a few weeks later it seemed to me that young Karol Radzio, the manager of our lumberyard, was giving me odd looks. One day he stopped me in the lumberyard and invited me for a couple of drinks. Now it was common knowledge among Polish Gentiles that Jews were much less given to alcohol than Poles, and that therefore if Jews ever did drink, they became drunk much faster than anyone else. I had a feeling that Radzio hoped a few shots of liquor would loosen my tongue and I would say something that would reveal my true identity.

Radzio led me into his room near the main office of the lumberyard. Astmuss, his only superior, was out of town on an inspection trip of other lumberyards. So here we sat, the two of us—Radzio, relaxed and well fed, and I, thin, undernourished and a little nervous. On the table in Radzio's room was a bottle of vodka with two glasses; also, there were two tea glasses and a platter of sandwiches filled with thick slices of Polish sausage. My mouth began to water; I had not even had a proper breakfast that morning.

Radzio opened the vodka bottle and filled our glasses. He kept refilling them and I did not dare refuse a refill because Polish officers had a reputation for their ability to consume large quantities of liquor in one sitting. And so, within a very short time, each of us had downed at least a pint of vodka. I was beginning to feel lightheaded, but I struggled to keep myself under rigid control and to watch my tongue. Actually, Radzio in the end was much more drunk than I and in no condition to ask me leading questions. Nevertheless, I did not want to take any chances. So, when we had finished our lunch and we went out together into the lumberyard, I pretended to be as drunk as a lord and talked loud and fast so that Radzio would have no opportunity to collect his wits and launch a man-to-man talk about my past. I started to curse the Germans, not in the manner of a Jew but in the way of a proper Polish officer and patriot who hated Hitler because he had humiliated Poland and robbed her of her independence.

Pela saw me on the grounds. She walked up to me, tapped me on the arm and led me into our room. The fire in our stove had been burning all day long and the room was warm and cozy. Perhaps the change of temperature from the wintry chill outside affected me; at any rate, I fell heavily on our bed and soon was dead to the world. All in all, the score had been in my favor. I had had my fill of vodka and meat, but if Radzio had planned our get-together as a "Jew-trap," he had failed miserably.

Our neighbors were very friendly. When Jasia had the chicken pox that spring, they brought her medicine and food. We were on particularly good terms with Adolf Lieberbauer, the chief bookkeeper, and his wife, Janina. Their son, Paul, became Jasia's special friend. The Lieberbauers, as far as we knew, took Pela and me for fullblooded Poles. So did the peasants, whom I made a special effort to cultivate because they tended to be suspicious of newcomers. I reasoned that if Pela and I could gain the trust of the peasants in the vicinity, I would not have to be afraid that they might report me to the Gestapo as a suspicious character. We succeeded in making friends with some of the peasants. One of them even engaged me to tutor his two sons in arithmetic. I was paid for each lesson with a bucketful of milk, fresh from the peasant's cow. Naturally, we gave most of the milk to Jasia so that it would make her healthy and strong. Much to our dismay, the milk was to have the opposite effect on our daughter.

When Easter came, Pela attended the festive services at the village church with the Lieberbauers and our landlords, the Nowakowskis. I stayed at home, explaining that someone had to look after Jasia, who was still recovering from her illness. The truth, of course, was different. I was still afraid of participating in a church service. Pela already felt completely at home at church because she had become familiar with the prayers and the worshippers' responses. But I was not so sure of myself. One Sunday, when I had accompanied Pela to church, I had the distinct impression that the other congregants were observing my every word and gesture. And so I resolved to stay away from church.

Three times that spring of 1943 Pela and I were poignantly reminded of the sufferings of other Jews and of the danger that we ourselves might not be able to escape these sufferings much longer.

Several days after Easter, a work detail of Jews from Treblinka I, the labor camp, was repairing the railroad track near our lumberyard. The camp inmates were closely watched by Ukrainian guards. But one of the prisoners managed to break away from his detail, came to our cottage and begged for a drink of water. Our neighbor, Roman Mamia's wife, happened to be standing in front of our door. She went to the well, filled a bucket with water and handed it to the man. "Drink as much as you need," she told him, "and then I'll give you another bucketful for your friends." The prisoner thanked her as though she had given him a bucketful of jewels. Then, without taking even a sip for himself, he turned and quickly walked with the bucket toward the tracks. But one of the Ukrainian guards caught him passing the bucket to his fellow workers. "*Herkommen!* (Come over here!)" the guard shouted, and when the unfortunate man placed the bucket on the ground so that he could obey the order, the guard kicked over the bucket so that all the water was spilled. Much later, the prisoner appeared at our door again to return the empty bucket to Mrs. Mamia. Pela, who saw the scene from our window, began to tremble and could not stop trembling for hours.

One of the cottages near the lumberyard housed a unit of Ukrainian soldiers, part of General Vlasov's infamous army of Ukrainians that had deserted from the Russian front and had gone over to the German side. This unit had been assigned to guard the surrounding area against sabotage from the Polish underground. Sometimes the commander of the unit "borrowed" Treblinka inmates working on the tracks and ordered them to clean his outdoor latrines with their bare hands while the Ukrainians stood by and watched with evident pleasure.

About a week after that—it was Saturday morning— Pela had her own personal encounter with an SS man. She had renewed the coat of red paint on our floor and had gone upstairs to visit our neighbor, Edward Mamia's wife, while the floor dried. Suddenly Edward entered the room. "Mrs. Bludovski," he said to Pela, "there's an SS man downstairs. Says he wants to see you." I was away at work. "An SS man?" Pela asked, trying to keep her voice calm. "I wonder what he would want from me." She was terrified but she could not afford to show it, not even to such friendly neighbors as Edward Mamia and his wife.

Pela went downstairs alone. "I want to have lunch here," the SS man said curtly.

"But—all I have in the house just now is potatoes and tea," Pela stammered.

178

"Never mind," said the SS man. "I've brought my food with me. What I want from you is just one cup and one plate."

Pela set out the cup and plate on our table, then asked the German whether he did not want some tea with his lunch.

"*Nein!*" the SS man replied. Then he opened his lunch box and a thermos jug of coffee. He placed a ham sandwich on our plate and poured some of the coffee into our cup. Apparently all he had really wanted was a quiet place where he could have his lunch. Perhaps he was afraid that any food the Poles might offer him could be poisoned.

After he had eaten he rose from the table and, with a curt "*Danke schoen!* (Thank you kindly!)," he left the house. Pela watched him from our window. She saw him heading straight for the railroad tracks; he probably was one of the SS men who had been assigned to help guard the work detail from Treblinka I.

In May, 1943, I myself met the Gestapo at first hand. Astmuss, the SS officer in charge of our lumberyard, called me into his office and handed me a large sealed envelope. "Take these papers to Gestapo headquarters in Lochow," he said. I stood rooted to the spot. Was I being ordered to walk into a German trap? Astmuss told me to take the afternoon train to Lochow. I went to our room and told Pela. My first impulse was that we should leave everything and run away from Sadowne. But Pela pointed out that this would be madness. If we attempted to flee precipitately, Astmuss would be after us and the truth about us would come out at once. It was less of a risk for me to obey Astmuss' order and go to Gestapo headquarters than to run away. And so I set out for the depot. As I kissed Pela and Jasia good-by I wondered whether I would ever see them again.

In Lochow, I went directly from the station to the Gestapo building. The SS man who occupied the reception desk had a face like a criminal serving a life sentence in a maximum-security prison. I told him that I had come from the lumberyard near Sadowne and had an envelope with some documents to deliver. He ordered me to enter, took the envelope from me, and then asked me for my identity card. He took the card, explaining that it would be returned to me later. In the meantime, I was to have a seat and wait for further instructions.

I did not understand. Astmuss had not said anything to me about waiting at Gestapo headquarters for an answer or for any papers to bring back with me. I sat in the reception room for over two hours. I could hear some men shouting at each other in German behind a closed door. I wondered whether I would ever get out of that place alive and under my own power. The man at the reception desk had taken my identity card. If his superiors were to examine it in detail they would be able to tell that it was a forgery and I would be lost. In that case, what would become of Pela and Jasia?

"Bludovski!" I looked up. A tall Gestapo officer stood before me. I leaped to my feet. He handed me my identity card, along with an envelope addressed to Astmuss. "*Sie koennen gehen!* (You may go now!)" he barked.

Once again, luck had been with me. I walked out of the Gestapo building with studied nonchalance, but once I was outside I started to run and ran all the way back to the station. When I entered our room in Sadowne and looked into Pela's eyes, I could see the agonized suspense in which she had lived that afternoon.

Jasia became sick again. She developed a high fever. Once again Pela took her to Dr. Stankiewicz, the pedia-

180

My son-in-law, Garry Brainin

1981: Joanne at the Women's American ORT Convention

Our grandson, Rickey Aaric Brainin

Our granddaughter, Rohanna Brainin, age 11

trician who had examined her the preceding fall. The doctor had bad news for us: Jasia had tuberculosis and would have to go to a hospital. Pela was stunned. In those days, and particularly under the unsettled conditions of our life, tuberculosis could be a very serious illness. Pela tried to figure out how Jasia had caught the disease. No one whom we knew in the village had lung trouble. Later, we traced our misfortune back to the milk I had received in payment for tutoring the two peasant lads in our village. The cow which had given the milk had become infected with tuberculosis and so the milk which was supposed to keep Jasia healthy had made her very sick instead.

Tuberculosis, Pela knew, was not the same thing as dysentery. She realized that this time she could not insist on keeping Jasia at home with us. And so Pela made no protest when Dr. Stankiewicz telephoned a children's hospital in Warsaw to arrange for Jasia's admission there. He made it clear to the admissions office that the child's father was active in the "movement" (meaning, of course, the Polish underground), and that he hoped the hospital would therefore accept the child free of charge.

Pela took Jasia to the hospital directly from the doctor's office. The thought of leaving our little girl in the care of strangers was almost more than my wife could bear. Quite aside from her fears for Jasia's health, she did not know how Jasia would react to being away from us, among doctors, nurses, and other children who would not give her the love we had always lavished upon her. Jasia was only two years old, too young to understand what was about to happen to her. So all that Pela could do was to hug and kiss her over and over again and assure her that we would come to see her as often as we could until she would be all well and ready to come home again.

Then Pela left the hospital and took the train back to Sadowne. As the train chugged through the Polish countryside she wondered how I would take the news about Jasia, and she began to cry. One of the passengers seated near her, an elderly woman, asked her why she was crying. When Pela told her that her little daughter was very, very sick, the woman tried to comfort her. "You're still a young woman, dear," she said. "If you lose this child, you can still have plenty of others to take her place."

After hearing Dr. Stankiewicz's diagnosis from Pela, I decided to go to Warsaw myself for a talk with the doctor. Dr. Stankiewicz explained to me that Jasia was in no immediate danger; the disease had been caught in its incipient stage. The fastest way to arrest the infection, he said, would be with injections of gold which would keep the pinpoint cavity in Jasia's lung from growing and give it a chance to heal. If Jasia could get these injections, she might be able to go home after five or six weeks of rest and good food at the hospital. The only problem, as he saw it, was from where we could obtain the gold. It had all been requisitioned for use by the German army medical corps. Of course, there was always the black market . . . .

I stared blankly at the doctor as he spoke. Gold on the black market would cost thousands of zlotys. It seemed to me like attempting to reach into the sky to pluck down a star. But as I left the doctor's office I was determined that nothing would be impossible for us when it came to the health of our child. Pela and I went to visit our wonderful Greek friend Mr. Kokkinakis and told him of our plight.

"Don't worry, don't worry," the old gentleman said. "I still have my friends. I'll get the gold for you." One of his friends who had connections with the Italian embassy in Warsaw managed to obtain the gold in standard series of five injection units. When we asked Kokkinakis how much we owed him, he said, "Nothing." As soon as we received the precious vials, Pela went to the hospital and gave them to the doctor. The doctor told her he hoped he would not have to use all the five units; perhaps three would be sufficient. "Never mind," said Pela. "Take all the five anyway. If Jasia won't need them, you can always use them for another child."

But there was still another problem. If Jasia was to recover without permanent damage to her health, she would have to have lots of good, nutritious food, and this had become a luxury even in the children's hospital. Once again, our friend Kokkinakis came to our rescue. Day after day, Anna, his maid, came to the hospital with delicious meat soups and finely chopped meat and chicken. Somehow she even got her hands on oranges, which were hardly ever seen in Polish homes any more because their cost had become prohibitive. The nuns who served as nurses at the hospital shook their heads in amazement when they saw the delicacies Jasia was receiving. They had been told that Jasia's parents were in the Polish underground and they must have wondered how it was that members of the underground, who didn't have enough money to pay for a hospital bed, always managed to get the best of everything. They made sure that none of the food was thrown out; whatever Jasia left uneaten each day was given to the other children in the hospital.

I think it was largely thanks to the good food sent by Kokkinakis that Jasia recovered as quickly as she did. She needed only three of the five gold injections and at the end of six weeks we were told that the disease process had been stopped and that Jasia was well enough to leave the hospital.

However, the doctor said it would be good if Jasia could recuperate at a convalescent home for another month or so. He suggested a sanatorium for children in Swider, a resort not far from Warsaw. This sanatorium, he told us, was managed by nuns. "Your little girl would be in the best of hands there," he said with a smile. Then, seeing the look of reluctance in Pela's eyes, his face became serious. "Frankly, my dear," he continued, "I do not think your little girl is ready to return home to you as yet; I know the unpredictable conditions under which you underground people must live."

But despite Dr. Stankiewicz's earnest advice we took Jasia home with us directly from the hospital. The hospital had been willing to keep the "little underground girl" free of charge, but a sanatorium was a luxury for which we would have to pay and we simply did not have the money. And so we took Jasia back with us to Sadowne, determined that our love and care would make her well. As an executive in the lumberyard, I started doing what my fellow executives had been doing all along: I gave extra shipments of lumber to the peasants who came to pick up orders, and I took my payment in the form of butter and cream for our little girl.

Much to our joy and relief, Jasia improved rapidly. Three years later, when we landed in the United States and were put through the chest X-rays required by law for every immigrant, the result was negative.

We had barely recovered from the shock of Jasia's illness when tragedy struck: We lost Walus Radziejewski, whom I had come to love like a younger brother. In July, 1943, he came down with the mumps, and his parents notified the lumberyard office that he would have to be absent from work for several weeks.

One day, during lunch hour, I saw a group of workers huddled together, exchanging whispers. As I walked on

184

toward the railroad siding I met Mr. Baran, the young man in charge of the "produce warehouse" near the tracks. I had never trusted Baran who, like his neighbor, the stationmaster Romanowski, had a reputation as a vicious anti-Semite. Now he stopped me, and with a doleful look on his face, said, "Mr. Bludovski, have you heard the sad news? The Gestapo just caught Walus Radziejewski and his mother. They killed both of them. They're still looking for the father. Somebody told the Gestapo that Walus and his folks were Jewish. If that's true, they sure had us fooled all along. You know, I'm kind of sorry about it. I always thought they were such nice people."

As Baran spoke, I felt as if a heavy fist had struck me a blow in the chest and had then moved on to my throat to strangle me. But I had to maintain my self-control because I knew that my life, and the lives of Pela and Jasia, depended upon it. I had to pretend that my interest in the news was one of mere curiosity.

"They're Jewish? Why, that's ridiculous!" I said. "Why should the Gestapo be interested in those people? Better stop spreading rumors like that." Then I turned back and quickly walked toward our cottage. I saw Mr. Lieberbauer walking from the office toward his house. His face was extremely pale. It seemed odd, but I didn't pay much attention to it. Astmuss was out of town (as he was now very often), at another lumberyard near Lvov, in the southern part of Poland.

The whistle blew, announcing the end of the lunch hours. We—Roman Mamia and I—started to work outdoors in the yard, measuring lumber. It was a very hot afternoon. I was tanned from working in the sun. I looked like a typical Polish worker, dressed in a shirt with rolled-up sleeves and work boots. As we stood among the stacks of lumber, we suddenly heard the roar

185

of motorcycles, cars and trucks. Before we knew it, the lumberyard was surrounded by the Gestapo. They came toward us with machine guns and started to search everybody and everything. First, they asked for identification cards. One of the SS men came toward Mr. Mamia and me. Mr. Mamia asked him in German what this was all about. It was none of his business, the SS man replied and ordered him to show his *Kennkarte*. Mamia showed him the card. Then the SS man turned to me. And at this point another miracle happened. I gave the SS man my card, but he looked at everything except the card. He handed the card back to me, then bent to examine the lumber as if he were looking for something. Finally, he turned away from us. I walked on toward the cottage. I saw Pela with Jasia in her arms coming out of the house. I wanted to tell her about my experience. In my excitement I shouted, "Zosia, don't worry! Everything is OK!" I immediately realized I had made a mistake. This outburst of mine could have had tragic consequences.

I learned from Pela that an SS man had come into her room also and asked her for her identity card. But he, too, had not paid much attention to it. He had merely looked around and left the room.

This Gestapo raid lasted about an hour. Then, without any explanation, the Germans left.

Eventually, from deliberately casual talks with some peasants, I was able to piece together what had happened to Walus Radziejewski and his family.

It seemed that Walus' father, Daniel, who had been producing corn vodka in partnership with several other Polish peasants, had drunk a little too much himself one day and, contrary to his usual gentle, refined nature, had gotten into a violent argument with one of his partners. In all likelihood that peasant had then informed the

Gestapo that the Radziejewskis were suspicious characters. Perhaps the peasants distrusted the fine manners and the elegant ways which the Radziejewskis had brought with them from Lodz. At any rate, the Gestapo had turned up in front of the Radziejewskis' cottage. Walus, recuperating from his illness, happened to be sunning himself on the steps of the cottage when two SS men came up to him. One of them asked him whether his name was Radziejewski. When Walus replied that it was, the SS man asked him, "*Bist du Jude?* (Are you a Jew?)" It seems that at this point Walus lost his nerve and shouted something in Polish to his mother. Supposedly what he said was, "Mother, we'll need our vials." The Radziejewskis had once told me that they had vials of poison on hand to take if they were ever caught. Either the SS men knew enough Polish to understand what Walus had said, or perhaps they saw that Walus was terrified. At any rate, they aimed their guns at him and shot him in the head. Walus died instantly. When his mother rushed out of the cottage, screaming hysterically, they shot her, too. Then they rushed past the two bodies into the house and ransacked it. Mr. Radziejewski was not there. The Gestapo never found him because a friendly Pole broke the news to him that his wife and son were dead; he insisted that Radziejewski spend the night with him at his house, and then, the next morning, he put him aboard a train for Warsaw. Daniel Radziejewski survived the war. He was saved by a Polish Gentile woman, whom he subsequently married.

From then on Pela and I were haunted by the fear that my co-workers at the lumberyard and our neighbors were beginning to suspect us; that sooner or later we, too, would find ourselves face to face with an SS man who would ask us, "*Bist du Jude?*"

It seemed that the Gestapo was becoming suspicious of all newcomers to the area surrounding our lumberyard.

The local Polish police received orders that every in-dividual who had settled in Sadowne in 1940 or there-after would be required to register at the town hall. For Poles who had nothing to fear, this order was merely another demeaning inconvenience imposed upon them by the Germans. But for Pela and me it was a new threat to our lives and the life of our child. For we heard that before being registered, everyone would be required to fill in a form listing not only his name and the place and date of his birth, but also the names of his parents, his grandparents, his closest living kin, and the parishes to which he had belonged prior to settling in Sadowne. Our home-made "Aryan" papers were very poor forgeries and would not be able to pass scrutiny closer than a routine check.

What were we to do? Pela and I concluded that we had two alternatives. The one would be to pull up stakes and leave Sadowne that very night. But we knew we would never be able to do that. We had very little money, so we would have had to take refuge in the woods. And that would have meant risking the life of Jasia, who was still recovering from her bout with tuberculosis. The second alternative was to take a long chance and improvise.

I decided to talk the matter over with Adolf Lieber-bauer, whom I regarded as a *Volksdeutscher* but whom, for some reason, I trusted instinctively. The morning af-ter the registration order had been announced, I went straight to Lieberbauer and said to him, "Mr. Lieber-bauer, there is something I must tell you. I do not know you very well, but I trust you. Somehow, I feel that you are an honest man." I stopped to catch my breath, then continued, "You see, because of my activities in the Pol-ish underground, my wife and I have been using forged identity papers. This could prove quite embarrassing if I went to register and the authorities were to start checking into my background. How do you think I should handle this problem?"

Lieberbauer gave me a long look before he answered my question. "My wife and I don't have to register because we've been in Sadowne since 1939," he finally said. "But I think that you and I are, more or less, in the same predicament. And the problem is not just that you have forged papers."

And then Lieberbauer's own story came out. Adolf Lieberbauer was not a *Volksdeutscher* but an assimilated Galician Jew. He had converted to Catholicism in order to marry Janina, a staunch Polish Catholic. Their son, Paul, had not been circumcised and had been raised in the Catholic faith. Before the war, the Lieberbauers had lived in Lvov, which once had been part of the Hapsburg monarchy. As a result, he spoke a fluent German. This, and his German-sounding surname, had enabled Lieberbauer to pass everywhere as a *Volksdeutscher*, so that even Astmuss, the SS officer, never questioned his origins. Even so, Lieberbauer had a problem. To the Germans a man born of Jewish parents, even if he had changed his religion, remained a Jew. This was the reason why the Lieberbauers had left Lvov after the outbreak of the war and had settled in the countryside where they believed they would be relatively safe from the prying eyes of the Gestapo.

After Lieberbauer had finished telling me his story, I told him the truth about Pela and myself—that we were not members of the Polish underground but Jews. Lieberbauer listened to me with great compassion and then gave me his advice, which I followed when I went to the town hall the next morning in order to register.

At the town hall, I asked to see the chief clerk, who was a Pole. I dropped our forged "Aryan" papers on his desk and said to him in a very firm voice, "Here you have the

Kennkarten for my wife and myself. These papers are forged papers. I have no other documents because we are members of the Polish underground. If you ask us no questions but register us legally, I will shake your hand as a Polish patriot and gentleman. You could, of course, refuse to register us. But in that case my comrades will come here tonight and blow up this town hall."

When I had finished, the clerk looked at me for a moment, then rose from his seat and shook my hand. "I congratulate you on your courage," he said. Without another word, he registered Pela and me as Adam and Zofia Bludovski, pure "Aryans," both of Russian birth but of Polish citizenship.

When I returned home and reported my success to the Lieberbauers, they were both elated. "You passed the test with flying colors," they declared.

And so we had won another reprieve from constant fear. It lasted exactly one month.

One day in August, 1943, Mr. Lieberbauer and his wife came to our room. They were very much upset. After I had closed the door, Lieberbauer pulled a letter from his pocket and showed it to Pela and me. It was a typewritten note mailed from a lumberyard near Lvov, Lieberbauer's native city, and it read as follows:

Dear Mr. Lieberbauer:

Several days ago the Gestapo was here looking for you. I had to tell them the place to which you moved. If you have anything to hide—I mean if you are not what you have been pretending to be—I would strongly suggest that you and your family leave that place and go somewhere else.

Sincerely,
A Friend

There was no signature.

Pela and I had to devise an escape plan for the Lieberbauers. I suggested that Mr. Lieberbauer should come
down with an attack of abdominal pain that very night
and leave Sadowne for Warsaw the next morning with
his wife and son under the pretext that he had to go to the
hospital. In Warsaw, they were to contact our friend Mr.
Kokkinakis. I would arrange that, at certain stated intervals, Mrs. Lieberbauer would meet Pela at Kokkinakis'
office so that Pela could keep the Lieberbauers up to date
on the latest developments at the lumberyard and let
them know whether, and when, it would be safe for them
to return to Sadowne.

The Lieberbauers accepted our plan with enthusiasm.
At 5 o'clock the next morning all three Lieberbauers
boarded the early train for Warsaw. From there, they
went to Otwock, the nearby health resort.

Meanwhile, in Sadowne, the Polish underground decided to teach a lesson to the SS officer Astmuss, and his
Polish mistress, Felicia. The local underground cell had
suffered a great deal of harassment and suspected that
Felicia, a frank Nazi collaborator, had been the cause.
So, at 2 o'clock in the morning of August 15, a band of
young Polish partisans broke into Astmuss' home. They
did not want to kill him for a start, but gave him and his
girl friend such a thorough beating that neither of them
was able to stand or sit for several weeks. Before they left,
the partisans warned Astmuss and Felicia that if either of
them dared to report the incident to the authorities or attempted to retaliate against the underground in any
manner, they, the partisans, would return and finish
them both off. The Germans whom I knew in the Polish
countryside were great cowards. They showed no fear
when they dealt with unarmed men, or with women and
children, but they dreaded the Polish underground,
especially when they found themselves outnumbered by

the "enemy." And so Astmuss and Felicia lay low and took no revenge.

Another few weeks went by. The Lieberbauers in Otwock were becoming impatient. They left messages with Mr. Kokkinakis that things were becoming difficult for them in Otwock and perhaps it would be safe for them to return to Sadowne now. I, however, kept sending them messages through Pela and Kokkinakis, begging them not to return but to inform Astmuss that Mr. Lieberbauer was still in the hospital with complications following surgery and that he would have to stay away from work indefinitely.

But once the summer season was over the Lieberbauers felt they could no longer remain at the resort. During the first week of September, the three Lieberbauers appeared in the lumberyard. When I remonstrated with Lieberbauer for having come back, he told me that the "ground had become too hot" for him in Otwock and besides, he felt that the anonymous note which had caused him and his family to flee from Sadowne had been nothing but a crude hoax.

Unfortunately, Lieberbauer was wrong about the note, for in the middle of September, the end came for him. It happened in the morning, while I was sitting with Mr. Lieberbauer in the office we shared. I was in the middle of a telephone conversation when there was a knock at the door. Two SS men armed with machine guns burst into the room. I had completed my call but was still holding the telephone receiver to my ear. I pretended that I was still talking. One of the two SS men remained standing at the door of the office. The other approached Lieberbauer and asked him in German whether Astmuss was in. Lieberbauer replied that Astmuss was out of town on official business (which was true).

"Is your name Lieberbauer?" the SS man wanted to know.

"Yes, it is," Lieberbauer replied, caught off balance.

"Then come with us," the SS man said.

Trying to appear as calm as possible, I put down the telephone receiver, turned to Lieberbauer and asked him in Polish what I should say if anyone were to ask for him while he was gone. When would he be back? Lieberbauer caught my cue and repeated my question to the SS man in German. "Tell him we'll let him know in good time," one of the SS men said to him.

After the SS men had left the office with Lieberbauer, I looked out the window to see where they were going. I saw that they were walking in the direction of Lieberbauer's cottage. Pela was in bed with a gall bladder attack. She later told me that some time before the SS men had arrived at our office, she had seen from our window two SS men approaching the Lieberbauers' cottage. This had not upset her particularly; she thought that the Germans might have come on routine business with Astmuss and, learning that Astmuss was away, had turned to Lieberbauer for help. Several minutes later Pela had seen the two SS men emerge from the house, alone.

I was able to reconstruct what followed. It seemed that, finding the house empty, the two Nazis had come to our office to look for Lieberbauer, then escorted him back to his cottage and ordered him to explain the whereabouts of his wife and son. Apparently Lieberbauer was surprised that Janina and Paul were not in the house. So he knocked at our door to ask Pela where they might be. Pela said she thought that the two had gone shopping. What she did not know was that Mr. Nowakowski, having seen the SS men walk toward our office, had warned Janina and had told her to hide in his attic with her son. Pela had not seen the SS men with Lieberbauer; probably they had been waiting for him outside, their machine guns poised in case he attempted to escape. But after Lieberbauer left our cottage, Pela looked out of the window again and saw the SS men pushing him into an army car. That was the last we saw of Adolf Lieberbauer. I do not know why the Germans were so much interested in Janina. After all, Janina Lieberbauer was an "Aryan." But according to the Nuremberg laws, her son Paul was a Jew.

When I returned home from my office, I found Janina and Paul Lieberbauer huddled together in the Nowakowskis' attic. Janina seemed stunned, unable to move. The next morning the Nowakowskis put Janina and Paul Lieberbauer on the 5 o'clock train for Warsaw. They sympathized with her, and perhaps even with her unfortunate husband, but, as they put it afterwards, they "did not want any more trouble in the lumberyard."

Pela and I were in a state of shock. Three families—the Radziejewskis, the Lieberbauers, and Pela and myself— had met by chance in the Polish countryside and found out that we were united by one common bond: the fact that (except for Janina) we were Jewish. Now two of these families were gone. Absurdly or not, I began to feel that the eyes of everyone in the lumberyard were now upon Pela, Jasia and me. Once again, I reverted to my state of apprehension, as if something inside me were poised for instant flight. I expected something to happen any day, and indeed, we did not have long to wait.

17

One evening early in October, 1943, there was a knock on the door of our room. It was Zielinski, the chief mechanic of the lumberyard. He held a bottle of vodka in his hand and from his gait and speech I could tell that most of the bottle's contents were already inside him. He staggered into our room and clumsily lowered himself onto one of our three chairs. At first he said nothing, but then he drew a long breath and came straight to the point.

"Look, Mr. Bludovski," he slurred. "I didn't know how to tell you this, so I had to take a couple of drinks to get my courage up before I came here. You see, it's like this. The people around here are saying that you and your wife are probably Jewish. Now me, I don't care what you are—Jewish, Chinese, Indian. I just don't care. You're nice people and I like you. But we've already had enough blood shed in this lumberyard. First the Radziejewskis and now that poor fellow, Lieberbauer. I don't want you and your wife to be killed, too. Please—for your sake I hope it's not true, all that talk about your being Jewish, I mean. But if it is, then let me tell you, as a friend, that you'd better get away from this lumberyard, and from this town, and do it fast." He said all this without stopping for breath even once.

I looked straight into Zielinski's face, trying to show no emotion whatsoever. Pela caught my cue. She turned to me and began to shout in a shrill, angry voice. "You see, Adam, that's what we get for sticking our necks out and for being good Polish patriots, working for the underground. Just because we haven't lived in this town forever, everybody feels they can poke their noses into our business. I've told it to you time and again, Adam: this is no good. You get no thanks for swimming against the stream. We could have been safe and comfortable in Warsaw with our families and our friends—if only we'd minded our own business. But no, you, the great idealist, the former officer—you couldn't leave well enough alone. All that talk about going into hiding in the countryside so you could work for a free Poland! Look what you're getting for all your trouble. You get accused of being Jewish. That's what you get."

Then, turning to the mechanic, she added, "As for you, my friend, you'd better tell those big-mouthed pals of yours to keep quiet. You don't have to worry about us: we're not Jewish. But if all these good people in our lumberyard keep spreading this Jew-talk about us the Gestapo will come and find out that my husband was an officer in the Polish army. Then they'll arrest him. But I'll still be here, and if they get my husband, then believe me, I'll personally see to it that our comrades will burn down the homes of everybody who spread those ridiculous rumors about our being Jewish."

When Zielinski heard Pela's tirade, he actually seemed relieved. His face brightened and he apologized profusely. "Please, Mrs. Bludovsky, you gotta understand. Me, I never believed for a minute that you or your husband were Jewish. And I'm glad you're working with the underground. I only wish we had more honest patriots like you, Mr. Bludovski. Then our country would be free again very soon." With that, he plunked his vodka bottle onto our table and invited me to take a swig.

After toasts to our good health and fervent avowals of friendship, Zielinski picked up his bottle, now empty, and staggered out of our room. When he was gone, Pela threw herself down on our bed and wept for a long time. Then she bent over the crib in which Jasia was sleeping and covered her with kisses. "Dear God," she sobbed, "whatever happens to us, whether they catch us or not, please let our baby live. Don't let anything happen to her."

Pela and I became increasingly sure that the time had come for us to leave Sadowne. But we concluded that flight was out of the question for us. We had no place to go. In Sadowne we had a roof over our heads and some food to eat. We could not risk Jasia's life by taking her into the woods. Winter was coming and we could not expose her to cold and hunger. All we could do was hope that if we stayed in Sadowne and acted as if we had nothing to fear, the rumors about our being Jewish would eventually stop and we would be left in peace.

But fate seemed to insist on keeping us in a ceaseless state of anxious alert. Several days after Zielinski's visit, Pela took Jasia to the market in Sadowne to do some shopping. I was in my office. The telephone rang and I answered it. I heard the voice of a woman who was working at the Sadowne post office. "Mr. Bludovski," she said, "I have bad news for you. The Gestapo caught your wife and child here in Sadowne. They took them away—where to, I don't know."

I slammed down the receiver and rushed out of my office. I leaped onto my bicycle (most of the key employees at the lumberyard had one) and pedaled to the Nowakowski cottage. I ran into our room, grabbed the revolver I had picked up on my flight from Warsaw four years earlier and put it into my pants pocket. The gun was still loaded. Then I got back on my bicycle and pedaled with furious speed along the highway that led from the lumberyard to Sadowne and the local Gestapo headquarters. I was not quite sure precisely what I would do when I got there, or even whether Pela and Jasia would still be there when I arrived, but faced with the possibility of losing my wife and child I was incapable of rational thought. All I knew was that without Pela and Jasia I would have nothing left to live for. And if this was to be my end, at least I had my gun with me and I would take a few Germans with me when I died.

As I pedaled along the highway I saw two figures, one tall and one small, approaching from the opposite direction. I shook my head in disbelief. It was Pela and Jasia.

My bicycle swerved and I almost fell with it as I got off. I swept my wife and child into my arms. "What happened? What happened to you?" I stammered over and over again. Pela gave me a look devoid of understanding. "Why, what should have happened?" she asked. It turned out that they had not escaped from the Gestapo; they had never even seen a Gestapo man in the village.

After having seen Pela and Jasia safely home, I went back to my office, picked up the telephone and called the post office girl. I asked her in pretty sharp language where she had heard that my wife and child had been arrested. She started to laugh. "Don't you understand a joke, Mr. Bludovski?" she said. I made it very clear to her that I did not consider such jokes funny.

One evening in December, Pela collapsed with excruciating abdominal pains. The pains became so unbearable that she began to scream. It was all very strange. As I sat by her on our bed, holding her hand, all I could think was: If she has to scream, I hope she won't forget herself and lapse into the Yiddish of her childhood. If she screams something like "Oy, Mamma," we're done for. If she has to scream, at least let it be, "Jesus and Mary." However, as things turned out, this was to be the least of my worries because Pela lost consciousness.

But the Nowakowskis, and even Roman Mamia and his wife who lived in back of the cottage, had heard Pela's screams and rushed into our room. Nowakowski's son, the young yard supervisor, got on his bicycle and rode into the village for the doctor. The doctor, an elderly man, arrived in a horse-drawn wagon and examined Pela. He said she probably had kidney stones. By this time Pela had regained consciousness and the doctor gave her a pain-killing pill. But the pill did not help for long.

198

Early the next morning I decided we had no other choice but to take Pela to the nearest hospital, which was in Lochow, only a few miles away. So I hired a horse and wagon, piled it high with straw, put Pela on top, and told the driver to get a move on. One must not think that the hospital in Lochow was a health center complete with able doctors and the latest in medical equipment. It was a small, primitive clinic housed in a small building. I knew that if Pela needed an operation, it could never be performed there. She would have to go to a proper hospital in a larger city, perhaps in Warsaw. But I felt that if I could get her even to this small clinic I would be much less worried about her than if she remained in our room where nobody could do anything to relieve her agony.

Strangely enough, when we arrived at the clinic Pela said that she felt a little better. The doctor at the clinic told us that Pela most probably did not have kidney stones but an internal cyst. The terrible pains had been caused by the cyst twisting on its stem, he explained. "But how come she has less pain now?" I wanted to know. "Maybe it was the ride from your home to the clinic," the doctor said. "The road is pretty bumpy. Perhaps your wagon jiggled and that cyst inside your wife got unwound again."

Eventually, the doctor told us, the cyst would have to be removed, but this was not the proper time for the operation because Pela was running a temperature. He gave her an injection and advised me to take her home again. "There's nothing more we can do for her here and we need the space for other patients," he said. "Take her home with you and let her stay in bed for about a week so she can get her strength back. Later, we'll see about operating on her."

Luckily, the injection helped. Pela's pains disappeared, and after a week in bed at home she was back on her feet.

Before we knew it, Christmas was here again, our second Christmas in an "Aryan" world. This time I accompanied Pela to Midnight Mass. My apprehensions that something I might do in church would give me away were blanked out by the conviction that the only way in which I could put a sure stop to the rumors about my being Jewish was by appearing at church together with my wife. And so I attended the Christmas service, watching Pela carefully and taking my cues from her. Thanks to the tutelage of Christina and Mrs. Slovik back in Zambrzyniec and her own frequent attendance at church, Pela had acquired all the "skills" of Catholic worship such as when to kneel, when to rise and how to respond to the chants of the priest.

The one visitor we ever received from outside Sadowne was Edward Galewski, who had arranged for our forged "Aryan" papers and who had escaped from the Warsaw ghetto with us. He had found a job in a neighboring lumberyard and visited my place of work on his business trips.

One day we told Edward about our fears of getting caught. He agreed that we had stayed in one place long enough. "Look, Adam," he said. "I think that at this point it would be safer if the three of you separated, at least for the time being. I've got some excellent connections near Warsaw, good Poles whom you could trust not to give you away. There's one family, for instance, who have an extra room in their apartment. Pela could go there as a maid. I'd find another place nearby for Jasia. With you, Adam, it should be even easier. I have the perfect place for you—"

I opened my mouth to answer, but Edward stopped me with a gesture of his hand. "Adam, I know how you feel about leaving Pela and Jasia on their own. But believe me, if each of you is in a different place you'll have a better chance of surviving now than if you stay together. You'll be able to keep in touch with Pela and with the family who'd take Jasia. Besides, you know it can't last much longer. Hitler can't go on forever."

But I rejected Edward's advice. I told him in no uncertain terms that I would permit neither my wife nor my daughter to stay with anyone I had never met. I would not let them out of my sight unless I could be sure they were in a truly safe place.

In January, 1944, however, I was forced to part from both my wife and child because Pela had to go to the hospital. Her abdominal pains had returned and it was clear to me that she needed more competent care than she could receive at the clinic in Lochow. One of the men in the lumberyard told me about a Professor Czyzewicz, who was chief of surgery at the *Szpital Dzieciatka Jezus*—the Hospital of the Holy Infant Jesus—in Warsaw. I had heard of this doctor even before the war, and I knew that he was an outstanding surgeon. I did not know his human qualities, but I feared that if Pela continued to go without proper treatment, we might one day find ourselves faced with a life and death emergency. And so I decided to take the chance and have Pela examined by Prof. Czyzewicz in Warsaw.

After examining Pela, the professor said that she should be operated on without further delay. I asked him whether the operation would be dangerous. "You're asking me the wrong question, young man," the professor replied. "You should have asked me what would be more dangerous for your wife—to have the operation or to go on as she is, with this huge cyst inside her abdomen. Why, it must be the size of a grapefruit. If we don't operate, there's always a chance of infection or even gangrene. Once that happens, the patient's fate is beyond our control. So I urge you to have the operation per-

201

formed as soon as possible—that is, if you want your wife to stay alive."

From the professor's words I realized that we could no longer put off the operation. But I also knew that the Hospital of the Holy Infant Jesus was not a charity clinic. Patients at this hospital were expected to pay for their beds and for their treatment. How was I to raise the money? I threw myself at Prof. Czyzewicz's mercy. I explained to him that I was at present without funds worth mentioning because I was a former officer of the Polish army in hiding from the Germans. The professor looked at me, then at Pela. He seemed to understand. "Don't worry," he said to me. "I'll operate on your wife myself, and I'll collect the money from you whenever you'll have it." I think he suspected immediately that we were Jewish. Later, I learned that he had given a room in his apartment to Professor Beck, a well-known Jewish specialist who had been the hospital's chief of surgery before the Germans came. Thanks to Professor Czyzewicz, Professor Beck survived the war.

A date was set for Pela's operation. Meanwhile, I was told to take her home. She was going to be admitted to the hospital only two days before the operation.

I took Pela back with me to Sadowne. Our security problem had been solved. Pela and I now had a legitimate reason for leaving Sadowne and staying away for some time. But what were we to do about Jasia?

We decided to do now what we had so firmly refused to consider doing after Jasia's discharge from the children's hospital: We were going to put Jasia into the convalescent home in Swider which Dr. Stankiewicz, the pediatrician, had recommended to us at the time. I told the nuns who managed the sanatorium that I was a former officer of the Polish army, that I was a devout Catholic working for the Polish underground and that I had no money to pay for Jasia's care. But now my wife would have to go to the hospital for a serious operation and I was desperately in need of a place where our little girl, who was not quite three years old, could be cared for until her mother was well again. If I could not find such a place for Jasia, I would not be able to continue my resistance activities, I said.

The nuns were wonderful. I do not know whether they suspected that Pela and I were Jewish, but they immediately agreed to accept Jasia free of charge. Once again Pela and I had to go through the ordeal of putting our little girl into the care of strangers. We left her in the ward crying bitterly but we knew there was nothing else we could have done and we tried to persuade ourselves that Jasia would be in good hands.

We informed our neighbors and my co-workers at the lumberyard that the three of us were leaving town for a while because Pela needed an operation. Jasia, we said, would be staying with relatives in Warsaw. The Warsaw ghetto had been liquidated months before; hence, if you said you had relatives in Warsaw it was ample proof that you were not Jewish.

Pela entered the hospital in the middle of January, 1944. She was placed into a women's ward with five or six other patients. In order to bolster Pela's credibility as a good Polish Catholic, our friend Edward Galewski gave her a little breviary to keep with her in the hospital, along with a religious tract entitled *The Life of Saint Theresa*. Pela placed both books on full view atop her little bedside table. Before the operation a priest came to her bedside to hear her confession. This was something for which Pela had not been prepared. She did not know the responses used in this sacrament of the Church and she was afraid that her ignorance would betray that she was not the devout Catholic she had made herself out to be. So, when the priest asked her whether she was ready to confess her sins she told him that she was in too much pain to be able to perform the act with the full concentration it required. The priest gave her a sad but understanding smile, made the sign of the cross over her and left. I only hoped that when Pela came out of her anaesthesia after the operation she would not say anything that would betray her as a Jewess.

The operation took almost four hours. Afterwards, Prof. Czyzewicz told me that the operation had been performed in the nick of time. Pela's abdomen had been full of pus. Had we waited only a few days longer, it probably would have been too late to save her.

Almost as soon as Pela was awake again the priest made a return appearance. He inquired whether she was now ready to make her confession. Once again Pela protested; she said she was still too weak and tired to concentrate on repentance. Very well, the priest said, he would take her deadly sins upon his conscience, but he would suggest that she at least attempt to confess her lesser sins. When Pela still refused, he shook his head, smiled and walked away. Pela thought he suspected she was Jewish, because he stopped pressing her about making her confession but gave her a friendly smile whenever he passed through her ward on his daily rounds.

Because her operation had been a difficult one, Pela had to remain in the hospital for seven weeks. It was during this period that Soviet planes first appeared over Warsaw and the patients were forced to make frequent trips to the hospital's air raid shelter. In her weakened state, Pela became so depressed that she begged the nurses not to take her to the air raid shelter but to leave her in the ward; she said she no longer cared what happened to her.

The food which Pela was served at the hospital was not the kind to cheer a patient or to stimulate her appetite. Most of the patients had relatives or friends who brought them home-cooked meals each day. Pela did not have this good fortune. Once a nurse gave her some soup left over by one of the patients who had received a delicious meal from her family, but this never happened again. Two days after her operation Pela asked for a cup of tea with a slice of lemon. The nurse explained that patients could not have lemon in their tea; lemons were too expensive. It was very depressing for me to know that I did not even have the money to buy a lemon for my wife's tea. I am sure that if I had contacted our friend Stomatos Kokkinakis, he would have sent Pela all sorts of delicacies just as he had done when Jasia had been in the hospital. But I did not dare turn to him just then. I had heard that he had gotten into trouble with the Gestapo for giving aid and shelter to Jews. In fact, he had been arrested once and it was thanks to his important Italian connections that he was released. I did not feel it would be right for me to endanger his freedom and perhaps even his life again by telling him of Pela's plight. As for the Piaseckis, they told me openly that they did not want to be seen in the hospital visiting Pela and that they would also prefer it if I did not come to their home too often.

Originally, I had planned to stay in Warsaw as long as Pela was in the hospital. But when I learned that the Piaseckis were not willing to let me sleep even on their kitchen floor I returned to Sadowne and commuted between Sadowne and Warsaw every day. It was a tiring routine but, given my frame of mind at the time, I actually felt more secure on the train between Sadowne and Warsaw than I did at the lumberyard. Every Sunday I visited Jasia at the sanatorium in Swider. I was happy to see that she, at least, was getting good food, that she had good color and had not only grown but also gained some weight. But these weekly visits to Jasia were emotionally exhausting because Jasia missed her mother very much and each time I left she would cling to me so that I had to pry her little arms gently from around my neck after kissing her good-by.

Pela's recovery was a long, slow process. For the first few weeks she had no visitors except for me. Then, at the end of her sixth week in the hospital, she received an unexpected visitor: the wife of our neighbor Roman Mamia. When Mrs. Mamia entered the ward, she found Pela reading the Catholic breviary which our friend Galewski had given her. Pela did this often in order to appear at least as devout as the other women in the ward who were constantly reading prayers or religious tracts. The Polish woman who occupied the bed next to Pela's took a great liking to Pela and seemed to enjoy talking to her. In one of their conversations she said to Pela that while she did not have any particular love for Hitler or the Germans, she was grateful to them for one thing: they had helped rid the world of the Jews.

I tried to put off Pela's discharge from the hospital as long as possible. I was not anxious to take her back to Sadowne. I had begun to inquire about positions in other small towns, but I did not know how soon, if ever, I would find another job. And so I stalled for time, hoping that a miracle would happen: either Hitler would come to a sudden bad end or the ideal position would become vacant for me somewhere deep in the Polish countryside where no one ever even gave a thought to Jews. Meanwhile, Jasia was safe in Swider; this was the one bright spot in our dismal lives. Pela and I felt that as long as Jasia was in the sanatorium she would be safe and well taken care of even if we, her parents, did not survive. I had given Mr. Kokkinakis, and even Mr. Piasecki, the address of my brother Henry in Palestine so that, if anything happened to Pela and me, they could get in touch with my brother after the war and send Jasia to him.

Obviously, Pela's stay in the hospital could not be dragged out indefinitely. We began to receive subtle, and eventually not so subtle, hints that it was time for Pela to leave. One day an assistant of Prof. Czyzewicz's walked into Pela's ward, stopped by her bed and informed her that she would have to leave the hospital without delay because she was taking up space needed for other patients. Pela promised him that she would leave as soon as I would be able to call for her, but she explained that he would have to be patient for another few days because I was away on a business trip. It was an excuse on which Pela and I had agreed. I purposely had not visited Pela for a number of days so that the doctors should not have an opportunity to put me on the spot and order me to take Pela away.

After the doctor left, Pela began to cry. Just then, Prof. Czyzewicz himself walked into the ward, followed by a half-dozen assistants, including the one who had just spoken to Pela. Pela was in the bed closest to the ward entrance, and usually, when the professor came in on his daily rounds, she would greet him with a broad smile. This time, however, she turned her head away because she did not want him to see her red-rimmed eyes.

But the professor noticed at once that something was wrong. He sat down by Pela's bed and took her hand. "What's the matter, young lady?" he asked. Pela wanted to tell him but stopped in the middle of a word because she saw that the assistant was standing nearby. Professor Czyzewicz, however, apparently guessed what was troubling her, for he said to Pela, "Look, my dear, I am the one person in charge at this hospital. If anyone here attempts to make things difficult for you, don't pay any attention. I'm the only person who can give the orders in this place."

Finally, in March, I could no longer stall for time. With a heavy heart, I took Pela out of the hospital and back to Sadowne. However, we left Jasia at the sanatorium because we felt that our own future was uncertain. We might have to flee from one place to the next and we wanted to spare Jasia as many hardships and unsettling experiences as possible.

Before we left Warsaw, Pela and I went to visit Jasia. Our little girl cried with joy at seeing her mother again. We spent that whole day with her and marveled at the atmosphere of peace and serenity which the nuns had been able to create for their young patients. In the evening, when we left our daughter, all the three of us cried, but Pela and I told ourselves that for the present, we had no other choice. The important thing was that, no matter what fate might hold in store for us, nothing must happen to Jasia.

Pela and I arrived in Sadowne after dark. I was glad, because I did not want too many people to see us at the depot or on the way to the Nowakowskis' cottage. The many months of living a lie, and now Pela's illness, had taken a heavy emotional toll: I, who had always proudly claimed not to be afraid of anything or anyone, saw an enemy lying in wait for us at every turn.

In our room at the Nowakowskis' I put Pela to bed at once. But Roman Mamia and his wife came to visit. They brought potato pancakes as a welcome-home gift for Pela. Pancakes were probably not the right food for her at this point but Pela greedily devoured them because they were such a welcome relief from the drab hospital diet.

Two days after our return to Sadowne I thought, once again, that the end had come for us. Astmuss, the SS officer in charge of the lumberyard, sent for me. When I entered his office, I saw that his face was flaming red; he seemed to have consumed quite a lot of vodka. He also seemed very angry. He shouted at me in his broken Polish, "Mr. Bludovski, listen to this! There are people working in this lumberyard who're trying to tell me that you are Jewish."

My heart failed. If Astmuss already "knew," then time had run out for me. I did not know how to answer him, but there was no need for me to speak because he kept on talking. "This is an outrage! A scandal!" he bellowed. "I don't ever want to hear such nonsense again! You're an efficient worker, and your wife is a nice woman. If anyone around here ever calls you a Jew, I want you to report him to me immediately, and I'll teach him a lesson he won't forget so soon!"

It was good, I thought, that Astmuss was drunk, because in his condition he probably had not noticed the look of terror that must have crossed my face when he talked about the rumors that I was Jewish. But now I was in full control of myself again. "I must admit, Mr. Astmuss," I said to him, "that to my knowledge this is the first time anyone dared to call me a Jew. Oh, well...I suppose there's a first time for everything."

But when I returned to our room, Pela and I knew that there was only one conclusion we could draw from my encounter with Astmuss: We had to leave Sadowne as soon as possible. And until we could leave, Pela and I would have to be constantly on our guard.

The following Saturday I took my bicycle and paid a visit to Edward Galewski. Although Edward and his wife lived only 18 miles away we purposely had not exchanged visits too often. It was healthier for Jews in hiding not to know too much about each other's lives and doings. The less you knew about your friends, the smaller the chances of your telling the Germans anything about them under torture. But this time I felt that I must see Edward. I told him that the rumors about my being Jewish had finally come to the ears of Astmuss and that I would have to take some drastic action.

Edward again suggested that Pela and I part and seek separate hideouts but I was not yet ready to do this. All I wanted from him for the time being was that he should obtain for Pela and me, through his underground connections, a new set of identity papers more official-looking than the crude forgeries with which we had been forced to make do ever since we had left the Warsaw ghetto in the summer of 1942.

Early one spring morning Pela and I were awakened by machine-gun fire. The shooting continued for over an hour. Polish partisans had attacked the Ukrainian army unit which was stationed near our lumberyard. The partisans had set fire to the "produce warehouse" which had been fairly bursting with farm products awaiting shipment to Germany.

The next day all the Germans and their collaborators in and around the lumberyard went about with downcast faces. The Germans were scared to death of the partisans. On the Sunday after the burning of the "produce warehouse" the partisans struck again. Astmuss and his mistress Felicia were attending a German wedding at an estate about ten miles from the lumberyard, at the edge of the woods. The festivities began at noon. At three o'clock in the afternoon a band of partisans emerged from the woods, broke into the great hall of the manor and aimed their machine guns at the wedding guests, most of whom were Germans or Polish collaborators. None of the guests attempted to offer resistance. As the

210

guests dispersed in confusion, the partisans ordered Astmuss to take off his fine leather SS boots (he had put on his uniform for the occasion), then stripped Felicia of her warm, fur-lined boots and ordered the couple at gunpoint to walk back to the lumberyard shoeless through the last of the winter snow. Meanwhile, other partisans gathered up the food which was still left on the tables and loaded it onto sleds which the guests had left behind in their precipitate flight. Then the partisans climbed onto the sleds and sped off back into the woods from where they had come.

From that Sunday on Astmuss and the other Germans in the lumberyard and in Sadowne were even more subdued than before. There were no reprisals against the partisans or against any of the other Poles in the area. Astmuss apparently believed that if he or any of his friends would try to take revenge, the partisans would put him and Felicia permanently out of action. The people in the village seemed to have no more interest in speculating about who in their midst might, or might not, be a Jew. All that concerned them now was when and where the partisans would strike next. The Germans were in a constant state of alarm; the Poles were euphoric. Good news had been coming of German defeats on the Russian front, and the Poles were certain that their country would soon be rid of Hitler and the hated Germans.

Pela and I worried whether we had been right to leave Jasia in the sanatorium. The Soviets had begun to bomb Warsaw and its railroad communications. What if we could no longer go to Warsaw to visit our daughter? What if the sanatorium itself got hit? Perhaps Jasia was now in no less danger at the sanatorium than she would be in Sadowne? So, just before Easter, we went to Warsaw to pick her up and bring her home again. Jasia was still a remarkably good and placid child. Much to our relief, she had no trouble making the adjustment from the sanatorium, where she had begun to make friends among the other children, to the confined, childless existence in our little room.

We were anxious that Jasia should be able to maintain the weight and strength she had gained at the sanatorium. To this end, we knew, she would need plenty of nutritious food. Despite the danger of the bombings, I decided to go to Warsaw and see what tidbits I could get for Jasia in the city.

Since Pela was still weak after her illness, I made several trips to Warsaw myself, explaining to Astmuss and Radzio, my immediate superiors, that I had relatives there who were sick and needed my help. Whenever I could do so, I avoided going to the Piaseckis. Better to make the homeward trip to Sadowne on a late night train, I thought, than to demean myself and seek the hospitality of people who had made it plain that they preferred not to have me in their house. But on one occasion I was forced to spend the night in Warsaw because the railroad tracks that led out of Warsaw had sustained particularly heavy damage in a bombing raid. I did not want to endanger the life of our old friend Kokkinakis, on whom, as I heard, the Gestapo was still keeping a sharp eye. So I had no other choice but to turn to the Piaseckis. They graciously permitted me to sleep on their kitchen floor. But the next morning they insisted that I leave their house at once. They did not even offer me a cup of coffee before I went. When they stepped out of their kitchen, I yanked down a chunk of Polish sausage which had been hanging by a string from the kitchen wall. I hid the sausage under my coat and left the house of my unwilling hosts. This was the first time in my life that I had taken something which was not mine. But I told myself that the Piaseckis had enough meat in their larder to last them at least for the next several weeks. So this little piece of sausage I had taken would make no difference to them, whereas it might do wonders for the health and spirits of my wife and child.

The rich, smoky aroma of the sausage made me feel weak and dizzy with hunger. But I did not take so much as one bite of the sausage, neither during the train ride home to Sadowne that night, nor in our room at the Nowakowskis'. Pela, too, refused to touch it. Instead, she cut it into small pieces and gave it to Jasia in daily "rations." I will never forget the sight of Jasia smacking her lips as she devoured the sausage and then licking the last bits of fat from her little fingers. I might have been a thief, but seeing how much Jasia enjoyed my loot made it all worthwhile.

By April, 1944, there was little doubt in our minds that we would be rid of the Germans soon. The fighting front was still several hundred miles away from our lumberyard but we knew that the Russians were advancing steadily. We had no radios, and newspapers came late and irregularly, but we received first-hand evidence of Russian victories almost every day as trainloads of wounded, weary and tattered German soldiers sped past our railroad depot in a mass retreat from the front. The Poles were not exactly happy that the Russians should appear as their saviors because they considered the Russians no more their friends than the Germans. However, as the old saying goes, in order to fight wolves you need dogs and so the Poles prayed in their churches for a speedy Russian victory. Pela and I, too, prayed that the Russians should come and drive the Germans out as soon as possible.

The people around us were now so busy discussing the war situation—the Germans with undisguised apprehension, the Poles with a glee they hardly attempted to conceal—that they seemed to be giving no more thought to Jews. Yet, I feared that this state of affairs might not last and that the Germans in the vicinity, perhaps in an act of desperate self-assertion, might go on a Jew-hunting spree and catch us before they went down in defeat. And so I continued looking for a job in another town in order that Pela, Jasia and I might be able to leave Sadowne.

18

One day late in April, a man from near Sadowne who frequently visited our lumberyard on business happened to mention to me that a building contractor he knew was hiring help. The construction sites were located near the railroad lines linking Siedlce, Terespol and Brzesc. One day, after working hours, I visited this contractor, whose name was Kniazew. Mr. Kniazew turned out to be a very nice person. He was of Russian origin. He and his family had left Russia after the 1917 Revolution and settled in Poland. Once again, I trotted out the story that I was a former officer in the Polish army in need of a job away from the big cities. Kniazew believed me. He and I took to each other immediately and he hired me as a supervisor. My job would be to travel along the railroad route, supervising the workers. My salary was to be much higher than what I had been receiving at the lumberyard. My base was to be in Siedlce, which I had passed in my flight from Warsaw over four years earlier.

I had no difficulty finding living quarters for us in the Siedlce area, which was quite a distance from Sadowne. I rented a room in the cottage of a peasant in Bialki, a village three miles outside Siedlce. The cottage had only two rooms: the one was occupied by the peasant and his family; the other was for Pela, Jasia and myself. This room, like the one at the Nowakowskis' in Sadowne, had one stove for both heating and cooking.

In order to make our departure from Sadowne as inconspicuous as possible we said no good-bys and made the trip to Siedlce by night train. We traveled by a roundabout route. At the Sadowne depot we bought tickets not for Siedlce but for another town. We did not want to risk having even the stationmaster of Sadowne know where we were headed. Only in the town which was named on our tickets and where no one knew us did we buy tickets for the next train to Siedlce. In Siedlce we hired a horse and wagon to take us and our few belongings to Bialki.

Pela and I immediately set about establishing ourselves in Bialki as Poles of pure "Aryan" stock. As she had done in Sadowne, so here, too, Pela made a point of being seen at church services and of cultivating the friendship of our neighbors. My own work schedule was such that I had to be on the road for part of each week. I was able to come home only on two days and Sundays. I devoted my three days at home to the task of helping Pela make friends with the people of Bialki.

Early in May, 1944, while supervising the construction of a railroad depot in Terespol, I met a Polish peasant who was to become one of our best friends. This came about in a small tavern near my construction site. It was late in the evening; I had worked overtime and had not yet had my supper. To my annoyance, the waitress informed me that there was nothing left to eat. All I could order was corn vodka. As I sat disconsolately at the counter drinking my vodka, a man with a moustache who looked as if he weighed at least 300 pounds sat down next to me. Somehow I felt that I could trust this man. So we struck up a conversation. The peasant said he was sorry that I had to go without supper. After a while he told me that he and his family lived near the tavern. "You could come over to our house," he suggested. "The wife should have a little food left for you." And I, who had come to suspect a bitter foe in almost every stranger, accepted his invitation. Perhaps it was the effect of the vodka, or perhaps it was a deep-felt need for a friend I could trust.

Uncle Tom—I never learned the man's real name— lived in a cottage with his wife and his stepdaughter, who was about 17 years old and was coughing constantly. Uncle Tom's wife invited me to sit down at the family table and served me a hearty supper: cabbage soup, ham, bacon, potatoes fried in plenty of lard and, best of all, good, home-baked fresh black bread. I had not eaten such a good meal since the outbreak of the war. I was only sorry that Pela and Jasia were not there to share it with me.

Uncle Tom was in an expansive mood. He told me all about his family. Among other things, he boasted that his parents and grandparents had lived to a ripe old age without ever having seen a doctor. I suggested that his stepdaughter, who kept coughing and looked rather pale, should break this family tradition because she was obviously sick. I insisted that he take her to a doctor or to a clinic to have her lungs examined. Uncle Tom took my advice, and it turned out that the girl was suffering from pleurisy. Her rapid recovery as a result of medical treatment gained me the gratitude and respect of Uncle Tom and his family.

As our friendship grew, I identified myself to Uncle Tom as an ex-officer of the Polish army. Uncle Tom in turn confided to me that he was active in the Polish underground and that his farmhouse was a contact point for members of the Polish resistance movement.

216

Before I met Uncle Tom I had slept outdoors, on the construction site, whenever I could not go home for the night. This was uncomfortable because it meant sleeping with my work clothes on. Now, Uncle Tom invited me to sleep at his house whenever I had to spend the night in Terespol.

Late in May, Uncle Tom suggested that I bring Pela and Jasia to Terespol for a week's stay at his home. That week was a true feast for my wife and child: they consumed huge quantities of fresh milk, sour cream, butter and ham.

It was at Uncle Tom's house that I made my first personal contact with members of the Polish underground. One evening early in the summer of 1944 I was present when a man of about 50 paid a visit to Uncle Tom. Although he wore peasant garb, it was obvious from this man's speech and bearing that he was from the city. When he saw that Uncle Tom was not alone, he was not sure whether it was safe for him to speak freely. But after Uncle Tom had introduced us to each other, he seemed to relax a little. At one point during the conversation Uncle Tom produced a cigarette and asked the visitor if he had some matches. The visitor took a small matchbox from his pants pocket and handed it to Uncle Tom. Soon after that, he said good-by and was gone. I noticed that he had left his matchbox on Uncle Tom's table. Uncle Tom opened the matchbox and pulled a tiny scrap of paper from underneath the matches. Penciled on the snippet were several numbers. These numbers, Uncle Tom explained, represented the date and the hour at which the partisans planned to blow up a train scheduled to pass through Siedlce with soldiers and munitions for the battlefront.

The spot near the tracks which the partisans had chosen for planting their home-made explosives hap-

217

pened to be one guarded by German soldiers around the clock. But the underground had plans for distracting the Germans. A short time before the explosives were to be laid near the tracks two young men in peasant costume turned up near the railroad tracks and staged a fistfight. They belabored each other not only with their fists but also with loud Polish curses. After a while one of the German soldiers left his post near the tracks to see what the noise was all about, but the two yokels did not seem aware of his presence: they kept on fighting and pulling each other's hair. The German soldier found the whole affair a great joke and called his partner over to watch the show. After a while the soldiers got the young men to stop fighting long enough to tell them what had started their quarrel. The two boys launched into a long recital, with many embellishments, about how the cattle of the one had persisted in invading the field of the other. They interrupted their tale at frequent intervals to continue their fistfight. This went on for about half an hour. Meanwhile, the underground had deposited its explosives on the tracks. Then the two wrestlers drew apart and walked away without a word, in opposite directions. An hour after the fight, the expected troop and munitions train passed over the spot where the explosives had been placed and was blown sky-high. The transport was a total loss, and many of the Germans aboard the train were killed or wounded. That same night Soviet planes flew over Terespol, dropping delayed-action explosives along with a contingent of parachutists who joined the Polish partisans in the woods nearby.

During this final phase of the war on the eastern front the Polish partisans became very active; each day brought new reports of attacks on German troop trains and military installations by partisan units. I frequently sat in on clandestine partisan meetings at Uncle Tom's home, but I never volunteered to participate in any of the sabotage operations. I would have wanted very much to lend a hand in anything that would hasten the Germans' departure from Poland, but not at the expense of my wife and child. I was certain that without me neither Pela nor Jasia would survive very long.

After a while my old fears reasserted themselves. I had a feeling that the people in Bialki had also begun to suspect that we were Jewish. Pela and I therefore made an about-face and took Jasia back again to the sanatorium in Swider, explaining to our neighbors that we were taking her to relatives in Warsaw. We visited Jasia as often as possible and were happy to see that, after the first few tears at parting from us, she felt completely at home again among the children in the sanatorium. We told our friend Uncle Tom that Jasia was sick and had to go to a sanatorium to be "built up" again. Uncle Tom and his wife were very sympathetic and frequently gave me eggs, sour cream and smoked meat to take with us when we went to visit Jasia.

Late in June, I made contact with our friend Edward Galewski to find out whether the new identification papers he had promised us were ready. He informed us that the papers were waiting for us in Warsaw, duly filled in except for the name of the place where I was now working. We agreed that Pela would go to Warsaw and pick up the papers at the home of our friend Stomatos Kokkinakis, who, Edward told us, had resumed his connections with the underground.

In Warsaw Kokkinakis handed Pela not only our new identification papers but also a batch of circulars which had been prepared by the underground for distribution in the countryside. The circulars announced the latest news of German military movements and of successful sabotage operations performed by the underground.

There was also an appeal calling on all Poles to cooperate with the underground in fighting against the Germans behind the battle lines.

Pela destroyed her old documents and inserted our new papers and the underground circulars into a pocket she had sewn into her girdle for this purpose. Then she boarded the train for the return trip to Siedlce. Once again, she almost did not come home.

On the way from the Siedlce depot to Bialki she stopped in a market place to buy some onions. Suddenly she heard the scream of sirens. Within minutes the market place was surrounded by Gestapo and SS men, some on motorcycles, others on army trucks and still others on foot. It was another one of the Gestapo's "manhunts" for Polish labor, much like the one we had experienced in the market place near Zambrzyniec in the fall of 1942. Half an hour or so before Pela's arrival, a Gestapo major had been ambushed and killed by members of the Polish underground and the Germans were out to punish the Poles. Pela later told me that there had been at least 200 civilians in that market place in Siedlce when the Germans struck.

After the Germans had encircled the market place in a tight vise of soldiers and armor, two Gestapo officers dumped the produce from one of the market tables. Another Gestapo officer bellowed orders into a megaphone that every Pole in the market place was to step up to the table with his or her papers ready for inspection.

Pela realized that if she were to be searched and the Germans would find the forged documents and the underground circulars in her girdle, she probably would be shot at once. But her presence of mind did not desert her. She noticed that, in the streets beyond the market place, outside the ring of German armor, traffic was moving normally, without any interference from the Germans.

So, if only she could slip past the Germans and dart off into one of the side streets she would be safe. Once again luck was with Pela. One spot in the German vise, only a few yards behind Pela, opened to admit a large black limousine, which drove straight into the market place. The driver leaped out, opened the rear door and three or four Gestapo officers emerged from the limousine. Obviously these men were of high rank because someone shouted "*Habt Acht!* (Attention!)" and all the Germans froze to stiff attention. While the Gestapo men concentrated on paying their respects to their exalted visitors, Pela slowly edged backward and suddenly found herself outside the market place. Turning quickly into one of the side streets she ducked into the first store she saw. "It's a manhunt out there again!" she panted to the surprised storekeeper. "I barely got away." The storekeeper took Pela's hand and pulled her toward the rear of the store. "Here's the back entrance," he said. "Go out through this door and you'll be safe."

Once she was out in the back street behind the store, Pela's first instinct was to break into a run, but she realized that this might attract attention. So she sauntered through the streets as if she were on her way home from an ordinary shopping trip. To her dismay she saw a German patrolman, accompanied by a Polish policeman, approaching from the opposite direction. It seemed to Pela as if the two were heading straight for her. From her previous encounters with the Gestapo—the one near Zambrzyniec and the other at the Praga railroad station — she remembered that one effective way of "neutralizing" the Germans was by assuming the initiative and taking them by surprise. Before the German and the Pole could come any closer, she marched straight up to them and with an innocent air asked them, in Polish, what time it was. The Pole gave her a broad smile and told her the time. She calmly thanked him; they moved on, past Pela, and Pela continued on her way.

Back in Bialki, Pela found herself a minor celebrity. She learned that she had been even luckier than she herself had known. For this time, in the market place, the Germans had not merely made random selections of Poles for deportation to forced labor camps in Germany. Thirty-five of the Polish civilians who had been in the market place at the time of the "manhunt" had been lined up and shot. Unable to track down the underground fighters who had killed the Gestapo major, the Germans had taken their revenge on Polish civilians.

By the end of June, 1944, the Germans in the area around Bialki were afraid to walk in the streets at night alone. On the battlefront, the German armies were in steady retreat before the advancing Russians. Train after train bearing ambulances and German wounded passed through Siedlce, which was about an hour's travel time from the river Bug, the natural boundary between the Russian and German sectors of Poland established in September, 1939.

Due to the steady Russian air raids, and the pressing need of the German army for rolling stock, railroad transportation for civilians had become erratic and difficult to obtain. Once again, we feared that we might be cut off from Jasia in the sanatorium. And so Pela made one more trip to Swider and brought Jasia home.

During all this time our company, under the direction of Mr. Kniazew, was building concrete air raid shelters for German soldiers and civilians near the Siedlce railroad station. But we had neither the proper personnel nor adequate building materials. As a result our shelters were not strong enough to stop a machine-gun bullet, let alone Soviet incendiary bombs.

I was able to come home from the construction site more often now. In retrospect, I think that Mr. Kniazew secretly suspected that I was Jewish, but in his view I believe this was an asset rather than a shortcoming in an employee. At any rate, he was more than kind to me, and when I told him that because of the air raids I was afraid to leave my wife and child alone so much, he gave me permission to go home as often during the week as I felt it necessary and even offered to pay my train fare.

With more time to spare at home in Bialki, I made it my business to cultivate the good will of the mayor of the village, a young peasant who was barely able to read and write. My connections with the mayor, of course, gave me added prestige in the eyes of the villagers and thus, I felt, would afford me some protection if things became difficult. A more immediate benefit from this new friendship was an opportunity to move my family to better living quarters. I found a large room at the home of a well-to-do peasant. In addition to the spacious homestead, this farm included a huge barn, along with a deep "potato cellar" dug in the ground which was covered with a wooden trapdoor and in which our new landlord stored potatoes for the fall and winter months.

As the summer of 1944 began we could hear artillery fire from the battlefront during the night. Soviet planes flew over Bialki almost every day. We heard that Brzesc, 70 miles of Bialki, had been taken by the Russians. The Germans were evacuating their military hospitals and administrative centers westward, in the direction of the German heartland. The work at Mr. Kniazew's construction projects came to an abrupt stop.

At the end of the first week in July, after several days of fierce fighting, Siedlce fell to the Russians. During the night of July 9 we could hear the roar of artillery and the whistle of bombs so clearly that most of us in the village, including the mayor and many farmers from neighboring areas, took shelter in potato cellars for hours on end. The cellar of our landlord was only about six by ten feet, but somehow two dozen people were able to crowd into it, standing up, almost suffocating beneath the closed wooden trapdoor. Now the gunfire was directly over our heads. Pela and the other women with us began to pray aloud in a vain attempt to drown out the sounds of battle above us. Even Jasia clasped her little hands: "Jesus!" she cried. "Come and help us!"

We spent five nights in the potato cellar. On the fifth night the thunder of the gunfire and the boom of hand grenades exploding directly above us were so fierce that we were sure we ourselves would be blown sky-high at any moment. As we stood with our arms tightly wrapped around Jasia and each other, we recalled the trials we had borne so willingly in order that Jasia might survive. Now I reproached myself for not having left Jasia at the sanatorium in Swider. There, at least, she might have had a chance to survive, whereas here....

Suddenly—it was about dawn—the shooting stopped.

Then there was dead silence. We held our breath. No one dared raise the trapdoor to see what was happening above ground. Three hours passed before one man mustered the courage to push up the trapdoor. Then the rest of us clambered out of the shelter after him. The village was a mass of smoke, rubble and smoldering wood. The farmstead on which we had lived was in ruins, as was the barn behind it. Horses and cows lay on the ground, dead. There was not one living soul in sight.

Suddenly, through the mist and smoke, human figures appeared: Russian soldiers, their faces and uniforms black with caked mud and dirt. Many of them were barefoot, but they all carried weapons. Then came German soldiers, looking as we had never seen them before: dazed

224

with the shock of defeat. They were surrounded by Russian troops. Some of the Germans carried wounded Russians on their backs, and their Russian captors prodded them on with their bayonets and beat them with their rifle butts to make them move faster. The once-proud sons of Hitler's master race, who had helped enslave millions of innocent people, were receiving their just deserts.

Pela and I looked at each other, still unable to grasp the idea that we were free at last. We solemnly kissed Jasia, then each other. With our daughter between us, clinging to our hands, we walked through the village to savor our first moments of deliverance. We passed the bodies of soldiers—German and Russian—piled upon one another on the ground. German prisoners of war, under Soviet bayonets, were clearing the rubble and the dead from the roads.

We had not eaten for the past five days, but we felt neither hungry nor tired now. Our hearts were bursting with relief. I looked at Pela. Her eyes were full of tears, but this time they were tears of happiness for all the three of us, that the terror had come to an end and we were still alive, together.

19

We were free, but we were homeless because Bialki was no more. Our first need was a roof over our heads. So, half-leading, half-carrying Jasia between us, we walked to the next village. There we found a farmstead which was still intact. Its owner agreed to let us stay there temporarily.

Late one afternoon as I walked through the village and watched the Soviet occupation troops settle in, I saw a

225

Russian officer who looked as if he might be Jewish. I approached him.

"*Amkha?*" I asked him. This is the Hebrew password which Jews meeting in unfamiliar surroundings have used for centuries to identify themselves to each other. Freely translated, it means, "Are you one of God's people?" If the person thus addressed was not a Jew he would not understand, and no harm was done.

But to my delight, the Russian nodded and repeated "*Amkha,*" then flung his arms around me in a bear hug. We talked in Yiddish. I told him that my family and I had been passing as "Aryans" for two years. He advised me to wait awhile before making it known to anyone else that I was Jewish. There was still the possibility that the Soviet troops might have to make a temporary retreat and the Germans might come back.

I followed the Soviet officer's advice for two more weeks, during which Pela and I remained in the village, living and acting the part of Polish "Aryans."

Early in August, Lublin, three or four miles from Bialki, was liberated by Soviet troops. On July 23 Soviet troops approaching the city had discovered Maidanek, an extermination camp in which a million and a half men, women and children had been gassed to death.

When we heard that Lublin was free Pela and I decided to go there. We assumed—correctly, as it turned out—that a city of this size would soon become a center for social and rehabilitation organizations which would help the survivors of the Nazi terror rebuild their lives. So the three of us hitchhiked to Lublin, mostly on Soviet army trucks.

In Lublin we learned that a chapter of the Polish Red Cross was already at work and had set up a temporary shelter for concentration camp survivors and other homeless Jews. Pela, Jasia and I applied for admission to

226

the shelter and were promptly accepted. Eventually, a "Jewish Committee" was organized to distribute food rations and clothing to people like ourselves. I offered my services to the "Jewish Committee;" I interviewed the refugees who were pouring into the city, helped them find accommodations and take steps to locate missing relatives.

Living conditions in the Red Cross shelter were quite crowded and primitive. We were housed in dormitories accommodating twelve to fourteen people sleeping in wooden bunk beds. Most of the refugees were in dire need of medical care.

In one of the dormitories there was a middle-aged man who had been to Treblinka and had survived. He spent most of his time on his bunk bed because he was very ill. After a while Pela noticed that whenever she passed his bed he followed her with his eyes. One day he motioned to her to come closer.

"Was your maiden name Miller?" he asked her.

"Why, yes," Pela replied.

"And your father—was his first name Aaron?"

"Yes, it was," said Pela.

The man burst into tears. "Pela, don't you remember me?" he sobbed. "I knew you when you were a little girl back in Warsaw." He had been an old friend of Pela's parents and had been at their home many times. Now he told Pela the story of his own sufferings. And then he spoke of her parents.

"I met your father in Treblinka late in August, 1942," he said. "What a sad reunion! I asked him where your mother was. He said he did not know. He himself had been picked up by the Germans in the street. He'd left your mother alone in their ghetto apartment. He cried bitterly; he did not care anymore whether he lived or died. He was sorry about one thing only: that he would

have to spend his last days on earth without your
mother." He paused for a moment to wipe his eyes with
the corner of his blanket. "Your father also told me that
you, your husband and your baby were in the countryside trying to pass as 'Aryans.' Oh, how happy he
would have been to know you are alive! He said that your
brother Ben had died in the early days of the war...."

So, all of our efforts to make Pela's parents believe that
Ben had escaped to Palestine had been in vain! Pela's
father had given up Ben for lost, and he and the mother
had spent the last two years of their lives mourning their
only son.

Pela looked straight into the eyes of her father's friend,
and he answered her unspoken question.

"No, my dear. No. Your parents are gone. So is Adam's
father. I was one of those who escaped in the summer of
1943. About 150 or so got away then, but your parents
and Adam's father were not among them. I suppose I
should consider myself luckier than most: I not only
escaped but actually survived. I think the Germans
caught most of the others in the woods and shot them.
Four of us managed to stay together. We joined a band of
Polish underground fighters in the woods, and we stayed
with them until the Russians came. Then I came here, to
Lublin. I figured that in this big city they'd know
whether anyone of my family was left.... But so far I've
heard nothing.... Nothing...."

Later, we learned that only about fifty of the inmates
who had escaped from Treblinka in August, 1943—following a prisoner revolt—had survived the war.

For days, Pela was close to the breaking point. Once
again, as in Zambrzyniec after I had returned from the
Warsaw ghetto without her parents and my father, I
feared for her sanity. But again, as she had done then,
two years earlier, she resolutely sat up in bed one morn-

ing and said, "Through all this terror I forced myself to survive for your sake and Jasia's. Now it's all over and we're still alive. I must not destroy everything now by losing myself. Jasia has a chance to grow up as a healthy human being in a new world. For this, she needs a mother who is alive and sane."

Pela and I were still worried about Jasia's health. We wanted to make certain that her tuberculosis had really been arrested and that she carried no other scars from our ordeal. We took her to a woman doctor at Red Cross headquarters. After examining Jasia, the doctor said that, considering what our child had gone through, she was in remarkably good shape. However, living at the Red Cross shelter would not be the best thing for Jasia's health. "You know that she is rather run-down," the doctor told us, "and so her resistance to infection is low. With the crowded conditions under which you are living here, and the cold season coming, you'll find her catching one sickness after another."

But what were we to do? The payment I was receiving for my work with the "Jewish Committee" consisted of nothing more than room and board at the shelter. But the doctor had an idea. She suggested that we place Jasia into a children's convalescent home which was housed in a convent near Lublin. She explained to us that, unlike the sanatorium in Swider, this institution accepted every child free of charge. "Of course, the generosity of the sisters creates a problem," the doctor added with a sigh. "Usually, every bed is taken. But I'll try and see whether they can make room for one more little girl."

We were lucky; Jasia was accepted by the sisters and remained there for the next four months.

That fall, for the first time since the outbreak of the war, Pela and I went to a synagogue for the High Holiday services. We had looked forward to this opportunity to reaffirm our Judaism together with other Jews who, like ourselves, had cheated death at the hands of the Germans. But at the same time we felt more than a little apprehensive. During the two years we had lived as "Aryans," Pela and I had sometimes wondered aloud what it would be like to resume our lives as Jews after the war, if we survived. It had never occurred to us to quit the Jewish community, as some assimilated Polish Jews had done even before the war, much less accept baptism into the Catholic Church. But now we asked ourselves whether our official return to the Jewish fold, symbolized by our attendance at synagogue services for the first time in over five years, would not trigger an emotional reaction greater than we would be able to bear.

The synagogue was packed. Here and there we saw men in uniform. These were Jews who had escaped into the Soviet sector in 1939 and had joined the Thaddeus Kosciusko Unit, the Polish liberation army which the Soviets had recruited from among Polish refugees. Now these men had come home to Poland and had met their fellow Jews again. I saw many of them weeping unashamedly; so were many of the others in the synagogue, mourning the loss of their families and the disappearance of a whole world which they had known.

As we joined in the age-old chants of the Yom Kippur ritual—Pela in the ladies' gallery and I downstairs with the men—we both felt our apprehensions drop away. It was as if, after two years of wandering, we had come home. We discovered in ourselves a deep-felt need to rebuild our lives not merely as individuals who had been placed into the world as Jews by accident of birth but as conscious members of a historic entity which for thousands of years had overcome seemingly insuperable odds against survival and which therefore had more than earned the right to live on.

In January, 1945, Warsaw was liberated. We took Jasia from the convent and went to Warsaw. During the long train ride, as I looked at Jasia sitting opposite me in Pela's lap, I wondered when and how Pela and I would tell Jasia the secret she had never known: that she was not, as the sisters at the convent had taught her, a child of Jesus, Christ but a daughter of the Jewish people.

When we arrived in Warsaw, we saw a city in ruins. We went to what had been the Warsaw ghetto, but we could not even find the street in which we had lived. The ghetto had been pounded into rubble.

It was clear that there was no place in Warsaw where we could stay. So we hitched a ride on a Soviet army truck headed for the resort town of Otwock. We thought we might stay in Otwock for a while because the climate would be good for Jasia. Almost as soon as we had climbed down from the truck, I found myself engulfed in a warm hug. It was a friend from the old days. He and his wife had survived the war, and they were now staying in Otwock while they decided whether or not to remain in Poland. He invited the three of us to stay in his apartment as his guests.

And so we left Lublin and made Otwock our home for the next seven months. I traveled to Warsaw frequently, made contact with the "Jewish Committee" there, receiving food and clothing for Pela, myself and Jasia.

I wanted to go to the Jewish cemetery in Warsaw to visit my mother's grave, but I was warned not to dare go there. The cemetery, I was told, had become an unsafe place. Hoodlums were hiding among the graves. No longer content merely to dig up the dead in search for gold teeth, they were now holding up visitors and, on occasion, murdering them. But these horror tales meant nothing to me. We had survived Hitler, so nothing could frighten us anymore. This was the cemetery through which we had taken our child out of the ghetto in a little coffin almost two and a half years earlier. I had not been at my mother's funeral, and at the time of our escape from the ghetto neither Pela nor I had dared stop to look for my mother's grave, but now I wanted to see the place where my mother had been buried. Pela, who had accompanied my mother on her last journey, recognized the area in which the grave was located, but to our dismay we found that the tombstones had been toppled and broken. No tombstone was in its proper place any longer.

Saddened beyond words, Pela and I left the cemetery and returned to Otwock.

Pela and I spoke of the future. I could not imagine our daughter growing up in Poland under the shadow of Communism. Unlike my brother Henry, I had not ever thought of going to Palestine before the war, but now I was eager to join my brother there. I was now convinced that if the Jewish people were to survive honorably, they needed a spiritual center. I felt that perhaps Palestine would be the one place where Jasia would be able to grow up without forever feeling the need to apologize for being a Jewess.

However, it was not so easy for Jews to go to Palestine in those days before the establishment of the State of Israel. The British still barred Jewish refugees from Palestine. Jews from Palestine—members of the Jewish Brigade who had fought alongside the Allies in Italy, and members of Haganah, the underground Jewish army— had come to Europe in the wake of the Allied victory to smuggle Jewish survivors across the borders of Europe and into Palestine, but this was difficult and often dangerous work. Border officials had to be bribed. Sometimes, transports traveled part of the way in vehicles "borrowed" from the Russians, the Poles or even

232

the Americans, but most border crossings had to be made on foot, under cover of night. I wondered whether the rigors of such a journey would not be too much for Pela or Jasia.

One day, at the office of the "Jewish Committee" in Warsaw, I found a letter addressed to me from Lodz. It came from Marian and Eva Rokacz, a couple with whom Pela and I had been friendly before the war. They had seen our names on a list of survivors and wanted to know our plans for the future. Marian and Eva had been lucky. Lodz had been liberated rather suddenly so that the city had remained fairly intact and our friends had been able to return to the large apartment in which they had lived before the war. In their letter they invited us to visit them in Lodz and talk things over.

We accepted the Rokaczes' invitation and stayed with them at their apartment for several weeks. I spent most of the time making contacts with survivors who had been leaders of Zionist groups before the war and who, I hoped, would be able to start us on our journey to Palestine.

Jasia still did not know that we were Jewish. Eva kept urging us to tell her, but here again, fear for the emotional well-being of our child held us back. We had no way of knowing what, if anything, the nuns at the sanatorium in Swider and the sisters in the convalescent home outside Lublin had told Jasia about Jews. We vaguely imagined that we would wait to tell her until after our arrival in Palestine, where she would not find it strange to be Jewish because everyone else she would meet there would be Jewish also.

But life has its own way of forcing confrontations. One day Marian, Eva, Pela and I went out, leaving Jasia in the care of Regina, a middle-aged Jewish woman who was also temporarily staying with our friends the Rokaczes.

Unlike Pela, Regina looked every bit as Jewish as she was: she had a dark complexion, a prominent nose and dark, frizzy hair which had only begun growing in again after Auschwitz.

When we came home that day we found Regina in tears. Jasia, she told us, had misbehaved. She had wanted to climb a ladder which happened to be standing in the Rokaczes kitchen. Fearful that Jasia might fall off the ladder and get hurt, Regina had told her to stay away from the ladder. At that point Jasia had turned on her and shouted, "You can't tell me what to do! You're not my mother! You're just a dirty old Jewish woman!"

As Regina talked, Eva looked straight into my eyes. "I think it's time that Jasia knows the truth," she said firmly. Then, seeing the uncertain look in Pela's eyes, Eva took Jasia by the hand and drew her down on the living room sofa beside her.

"I want you to tell me something, Jasia," she began. "Why did you call Regina a dirty old Jewish woman?"

Jasia fidgeted. "Because...because that's what she is. A dirty old Jewish woman, dirty old Jewish woman," she said in a little-girl chant.

"Look at me, Jasia," Eva persisted. "What would you say if I told you that you were Jewish, too?"

Jasia's eyes grew wide with amazement. "But I'm not Jewish!" she pouted, "I'm not!"

"But it's true, darling," Eva said gently. "You are Jewish. Your father and your mother are Jewish too."

Jasia burst into tears. "That's a dirty lie! My Mama and Daddy aren't Jewish!"

"What makes you so sure they aren't?" Eva wanted to know.

"Because they don't have ugly black hair like Regina, and their faces aren't dark and their noses aren't big...."

Eva rose from her couch and drew up Jasia with her. Once again, her eyes caught mine and held them. "Jasia," she said, "I think your Daddy wants to tell you something...."

Jasia walked over to me. She looked first at me, then turned to look at Pela. "Daddy, tell Aunt Eva she's lying! Tell her we aren't Jewish!"

Pela knelt down and drew Jasia close. "Darling—look at me, please," she said, then continued in a low voice. "Aunt Eva is not lying. You are Jewish. So are Daddy and I. You remember, don't you, how unhappy we were when we saw the German soldiers? We were unhappy because the German soldiers were bad people. They didn't like the Jews and so they wanted to kill them, just like the old witch who wanted to kill Hansel and Gretel. But we didn't want the German soldiers to kill you. We loved you too much. So your Daddy and I played a game of make-believe. We pretended that we were Christians, and that you were Christian, too, so that the Germans would leave you alone. That's why we are still here, together, and now we don't have to play make-believe anymore."

Jasia turned her face away from Pela's. "But I don't want to be Jewish!" she protested. "The sisters at the convent—they said that only Christians can pray to Jesus. If I'm Jewish, I won't be able to pray to Jesus and he won't love me anymore."

Pela tried to restrain Jasia, but Jasia pushed away her arms and ran into our room. We heard her lock herself in; then came bitter sobs. We knocked on the door and begged her to come out, but she did not seem to hear. She did not emerge until supper time. When she came out of our room she was no longer crying but seemed deep in thought. She opened her little fist and held out her hand to Pela. On her palm lay the dainty necklace with the gold cross she had worn ever since Mr. Kokkinakis' maid had first clasped it around her neck.

"If I'm not a Christian I can't wear this anymore, can I?" she asked her mother. Then, after a while, she turned to me with big, questioning eyes. "But if I can't pray to Jesus anymore, tell me, to whom am I supposed to pray?"

Pela drew Jasia into her arms. "Why, darling, you can still pray to God. All Jews pray to God. So do Christians. It's just that the Christians also pray to Jesus. Jews don't pray to Jesus. They pray only to God."

For some moments Jasia remained pensive. Then she tilted her palm and dropped the necklace with the cross into Pela's hand. "This is supposed to stand for Jesus, isn't it?" she asked. "If Jesus isn't my God anymore, then where is my God? Mama, please let me have my God!"

Pela gently explained to her that Jews did not need a cross or any other figure to remind them of God. However, the Jews did have a beautiful star called the Star of David. "When we get to Palestine, darling, we'll buy you a little necklace with the most beautiful Star of David any little girl ever had," Pela promised our daughter. We still have Jasia's little cross, tucked away in a drawer of keepsakes, to remind us of our two years as "Aryans."

Several days after this incident, we returned to Warsaw. I was increasingly anxious to leave Poland. The months passed very quickly. Then, in the early fall, I learned from my Zionist friends that a group of Jews who were scheduled to leave Poland for Palestine in October could take one more family. This group would travel through Czechoslovakia into West Germany, where they would enter a displaced persons' camp near Munich. There, they would meet with other small groups of Jews and eventually go on with them to Palestine via France or Italy.

So, one day at the end of October, 1945, Pela, Jasia and I boarded a train for Katowice with about 20 other Jews—young men, young women and a few children. We were escorted by a group leader who told us he had come to Poland from a kibbutz in Palestine to help rescue Jews from Poland. In Katowice, he produced an officer who wore the uniform of a major in the Red Army. But there was something strange about this major's behavior, for he loaded us all into a Russian military ambulance and took the driver's wheel himself.

A few hours later, the ambulance came to a stop. "Everybody out!" our escort said, opening the door. "We're inside the Czechoslovak border now." We climbed out of the ambulance and found ourselves at a small railroad station. "We'll wait for the next train to Prague," our escort told us as the ambulance, with the man in Russian uniform still at the wheel, drove away empty.

Unfortunately, on the train, there was a hitch. At one of the stops, Soviet military police boarded the train and placed us under arrest for having entered Czechoslovakia illegally. When the train stopped on the outskirts of Prague, the police took us off and locked us up in what looked like a huge barn. We stayed there overnight. The next morning the gates of the barn flew open and several Czech policemen entered. "You can come out now," they said in Polish. The Russians had disappeared. The Czech policemen were kindhearted fellows. They apparently understood our plight, for they escorted us to a train which took us to a point very close to the border between Czechoslovakia and West Germany.

That night—I think it was the last night in October—we crossed the border on foot into West Germany. The only possessions we had brought with us were the clothes on our backs. We had taken no other baggage

237

because we had been warned that we would have to ne-
gotiate difficult terrain on foot. I held Jasia, who was fast
asleep. Pela walked ahead of us.

Our march from Czechoslovakia into West Germany
took us almost all night. We were desperately tired but
the thought of freedom waiting for us on the other side of
the border gave us strength. Suddenly we heard a voice
shouting in English, "Halt! Who goes there?" We heaved
a sigh of relief. We had entered the American zone of
West Germany. Our escort, who spoke some English, explained to the American border patrolman that we were
refugees from Eastern Europe. We were permitted to
pass and directed to the nearest railroad station where
we could board a train bound for Munich.

From Munich we were driven directly to the displaced
persons' camp in Feldafing, where we were supposed to
await the next stage of our journey to Palestine via
France or Italy.

At the displaced persons' camp we were placed into
the basement of a large villa which had been confiscated
from a Nazi bigwig and which was now occupied by
about 60 other refugees.

Because I knew a little English from my high school
days in Warsaw I was assigned to work in the camp office. My supervisor there was Mrs. Dembitzer, an attrac-
tive young woman in her forties. A psychologist, she had
been born in France and had married a wealthy Belgian
diamond dealer. Just before the outbreak of the war, the
Dembitzers had emigrated to the United States and had
settled in New York. There, Mr. Dembitzer had made a
new start in the diamond business and soon was as
wealthy in New York as he had been in Belgium. Since
the Dembitzers had no children, Mrs. Dembitzer became
active in Jewish communal work. When the war ended,
she wanted to do "something useful," as she put it, and

asked her husband to let her go to Germany to work in a displaced persons' camp for a year. Mr. Dembitzer, who was considerably older than his wife, had no objections. That is how Pela, Jasia and I first met the lady with the French accent whom we came to call affectionately "Mamo" Dembitzer and who remained our best friend in the United States until her death in 1972.

When we first arrived at the displaced persons' camp we assumed that we would be moved on to France or Italy in a matter of weeks. But months went by and somehow our names never appeared on the list for the next outbound transport. Perhaps *B'riha* ("Flight"), as the movement for illegal immigration into Palestine had become known by that time, had received orders from its top command to give first priority to single young people or to young couples without small children. At any rate, the year 1945 had passed, it was now spring, 1946, and we were still in Feldafing.

One day in April, 1946 "Mamo" Dembitzer called me into her office and asked me whether I wanted to go to the United States. If so, she said, she could get papers for us immediately, and we could be out of the camp by the following Sunday.

I did not know what answer to give "Mamo" Dembitzer. Pela and I were still hoping for notification any day that we would be on the next transport bound for Palestine. On the other hand, we realized that we could not remain in a displaced persons' camp indefinitely, marking time and living on the bounty of others instead of taking active steps to build a new life for ourselves and Jasia.

"Mamo" Dembitzer understood my problem.

"I understand very well that you would like to go to join your brother in Palestine," she said. "However, I do believe that it is in your best interest not to make the

239

journey to Palestine from here. You should not expose your little girl to more hardships and dangers—more illegal border crossings—and then the trip across the Mediterranean! The 'illegal' ships are overloaded death traps! What if your boat sinks in the middle of the sea? Or if it is stopped by the British Navy and everyone aboard is either sent back to Germany or interned in some remote British colony? On the other hand, you must realize that it may take years before Jews will be able to enter Palestine legally. The British are not about to lift the ban on Jewish immigration. Someday there may be an independent Jewish state in Palestine to which any Jew will be able to immigrate without difficulty, but who knows when that will be? I don't want to see you vegetate here, in a displaced persons' camp, waiting for miracles to happen."

"Mamo" Dembitzer stopped for a moment, then smiled a little as she continued. "All right, let's assume that tomorrow you will be notified that you can proceed to Palestine with a *B'riha* transport, and you and your wife are willing to take the chance with your child. What if you arrive in Palestine only to find that you, or your wife, cannot stand the climate, or the hardships, or the economic situation? You know you can't enter the United States any time you feel like it. Now you have an immediate opportunity to go to America. I suggest you take advantage of this opportunity. See how you like life in the United States. If, after a few years in America, you'll still want to go to Palestine, it may be easier for you to go to Palestine from the United States than to go to the United States from Palestine."

I talked the matter over with Pela. She seemed to agree with "Mamo" Dembitzer's view of our situation. We informed "Mamo" Dembitzer that we would take her advice and were ready to leave for the United States.

240

We did not have much packing to do. I bartered a few packs of American cigarettes for a cardboard suitcase and a hatbox, piled our few belongings into these, and we were ready to set out for the New World.

We went to Munich where we waited for the next displaced persons' ship to sail for New York. Two weeks later we left Munich for Bremerhaven to board the SS *Marine Perch*, one of the transport ships set aside by the United States Navy for the transportation of displaced persons from Germany to the United States.

The Atlantic crossing took us twelve days. I slept in a dormitory filled with other men. Pela and Jasia were more fortunate. They shared a stateroom with only one woman, who was traveling with her little girl.

We landed in New York harbor in the evening of May 23, 1946 but we had to remain on the boat until the next morning, when the United States immigration officials came on board to clear us. It was a warm spring night, and we were too excited to go to sleep. Pela, Jasia and I stood on deck, looking at the lights of New York and at the Statue of Liberty with her torch raised high to welcome us. From far off we heard the wail of a siren: it may have been a police car, or perhaps an ambulance. Hearing the siren, Jasia became frightened and clung to Pela's skirt. "Mama, are they going to shoot us?" she wanted to know.

Pela smiled and pointed to the Statue of Liberty. "No, my darling," she said softly. "This is the land of freedom. They don't shoot people here."

Then Pela looked at me, embraced me and burst into tears. "I can't believe it," she sobbed. "We're here in America." "Didn't I tell you that we should never give up?" I said. "AFTER ALL, THERE'S ALWAYS TIME TO DIE."

20

Soon after our arrival in Chicago I had written down, in rudimentary form, the story of our lives between 1939 and 1945. Now, a generation later, I felt able at last to review what I had jotted down in those early days and to elaborate upon the memories which Pela and I share.

In the course of the years, particularly during the past decade, hundreds of Holocaust survivors have published accounts of their sufferings under the Hitler terror. They have been doing this because they are aware that they are no longer young, that their ranks are thinning and that they owe future generations an eyewitness history of a past which, in retrospect, almost defies credence.

Basically, I, too, was motivated by these considerations. But I was guided also by a more positive purpose. I want my grandchildren's generation to understand that mighty force which maintained in life so many of us who otherwise could have died or would have broken under the burden of subsisting for years as fugitives in perpetual flight and hiding: the love and devotion between husbands and wives, parents and children. We endeavored to survive not so much for our own sake as for the purpose of upholding one another.

Pela and I hope that these ties of mutual, self-sacrificing love may sustain also our children, and their children in turn, in a world better than the one which we, their parents, have known.